I'VE HAD IT UP TO HERE WITH
TEENAGERS

ALSO BY MELINDA RAINEY THOMPSON

SWAG: Southern Women Aging Gracefully
The SWAG Life
I Love You—Now Hush (with Morgan Murphy)

I'VE HAD IT UP TO HERE WITH
TEENAGERS

MELINDA RAINEY THOMPSON

JOHN F. BLAIR PUBLISHER
Winston-Salem, North Carolina

Published by

JOHN F. BLAIR
P U B L I S H E R
1406 Plaza Drive
Winston-Salem, North Carolina 27103
www.blairpub.com

COVER IMAGE

© H. ARMSTRONG ROBERTS/ClassicStock/Corbis

Cover design by Brooke Csuka
Interior by Debra Long Hampton and Morgan Hawk

Library of Congress Cataloging-in-Publication Data

Thompson, Melinda Rainey, 1963-
 I've had it up to here with teenagers / by Melinda Rainey Thompson.
    p.   cm.
 ISBN 978-0-89587-569-3 (alk. paper) — ISBN 978-0-89587-570-9 (ebook) 1.
Parent and teenager—Humor. I. Title.
 PN6231.P2T47 2012
 306.87402'07—dc23
                        2011042558

10 9 8 7 6 5 4 3 2 1

To my three teenagers:
Warner, Nat, and Lily.

I love you more than my next breath.

═══ Contents

TEENS ON THE LOOSE

A Letter from the Author

Dear Reader,

Writing books is the most fun job in the world. No question about it. Thank you from the bottom of my heart for reading my books. As long as you continue to read, I get to keep writing.

Is there anything I can get you, by the way? I really am very grateful.

The most important job I'll ever do in my life is to rear my children well. So far, they're turning out nicely. They're good kids. I like them. Other people do, too. I love them with a depth and breadth that frightens me sometimes. They're no trouble for anyone but me. That's the truth. It is also true that they make me absolutely nuts on a fairly regular basis.

Because I am a mean mama, not one of those sweet mamas, I thought long and hard before writing this book. I knew that if I ever decided to "go there," it wouldn't be pretty. I write humorous essays. That means I use stories from my real life. I don't get out that much. The humor in my books has always been at my expense, no one else's. This time, the humor is a little bit at my teenagers' expense, too. It is possible that I enjoyed writing this book a little too much. For months, when people asked my kids, "Is your mom writing another book?" they answered, "Yeah, she's writing a *revenge* book about teenagers." This response was accompanied by a teenage eye roll, of course.

I'm not sure what my teenagers are going to think when this book hits the shelves. I gave each of them the opportunity to read the manuscript beforehand and the option to remove anything they found particularly embarrassing, but mostly they were too busy to bother. They may live to regret that. My older son asked to write a rebuttal, which appears at the end of the book. That seemed fair to me. After all, I got to go first.

I hope that you enjoy reading about my very ordinary life. Every day offers moments of joy and sorrow. I bet my life is a lot like yours. Laughing at my highs and lows is sure to make you feel better about your own parenting. I guarantee it. We're all in this together, you know.

As always, I hope you find your life in these pages and laugh out loud. That's why I wrote this book.

All best wishes,

Melinda Rainey Thompson

LIFE LESSONS

What's with the Attitude?

Teenagers know everything. If you are unaware of this well-known fact, then I can only assume you do not currently live with, nor have you ever lived with, anyone between the ages of thirteen and nineteen. In teenagers' minds, their omniscience is a given. On teenager Fantasy Island, the converse is also true. Grownups know nothing at all. According to kids, we're all dumb as dirt. This premise is well established in households throughout the country and, for all I know, the world. I've heard we parents smarten up again when our kids hit their early twenties. I look forward to that. It'll be a nice change to have my wise counsel occasionally appreciated. These days, I receive eye rolls, deep sighs, and dramatic protests in return for my you-better-listen-to-what-I'm-telling-you-because-you're-going-to-need-this-information-later sermons.

In their minds, no one else has ever been a teenager before in the history of the world, so we cannot possibly understand the intricate complexities of their social lives. We know-nothing parents couldn't possibly have had similar problems or experiences when we were young. I am not sure our kids are convinced we were ever actually their age. They simply can't imagine it. It's beyond their ken. I suppose they think we were born old, fat, wrinkled, farsighted, and boring. Certainly, they can't imagine us dating. At the most, my kids may see the rare peck on the lips between my husband and me. (Who has the time, energy, or privacy for more than that? Tell the truth: if you have an extra hour and a kid-free house, which do you pick, a nap or a romantic interlude? Nap, right?) Their reaction is to close their eyes and say, "Gross!" Apparently, any public display of affection between people over the age of forty makes teenagers physically ill. It's just another way they make the grownups in their lives feel special.

I have watched the thoughts flitter across my teens' expressive faces on more than one occasion and read the message loud and clear: my teenagers think I am too stupid to live. That's not true. I'm not stupid, by God, and I have the degrees to prove it. It irritates me to no end to be condescended to by teenagers. When my daughter had the gall to say to me out loud one day, "What do you know about it?" in the middle of a heated discussion about boys and girls and the birds and the bees, my answer flew out of my mouth without a second's hesitation: "I know *plenty*, missy!" Then I stalked out of the room in a huff, just like a teenage girl (which I used to be, contrary to popular belief).

If I had to pick the one thing that annoys me most about living with teenagers—which I admit would be hard to do because the competition for that slot is tough and varies from day to day, depending upon who or what has set me off most recently—I would have to say that it is the classic teenage attitude toward . . . everything. Sometimes, it's not so much the words they choose; it's the tone in which they mutter those words under their breath. Most teenagers are too cool for school. The cockiness is usually not even a millimeter thick, of course. They can be brought down to earth in seconds with a few well-chosen words. Whoever said, "Sticks and stones may break my bones, but words will never hurt me," didn't have my vocabulary.

Even the most personable teenagers rarely allow themselves to display the excitement they revealed all the time as children. It's as if they've all taken some kind of pledge.

1. Don't show too much excitement, no matter how tempted you are to rave over something. An overt display of excitement gives grownups a big head.

2. Even if you are okay with a plan suggested by a grownup, complain about it. It's just good form.

3. Even if you still occasionally enjoy going places or doing things with your parents, don't tell them. They don't need to know everything. They just think they do.

4. Avoid sitting with your parents in public settings, even if you have to sit alone. Too much voluntary interaction between the generations is creepy.

5. Never do something the first time your parents ask. It makes you look overeager.

6. Keep communication with your parents to the bare

minimum. Respond primarily with indistinguishable grunts and monosyllables.

7. Initiate chatty conversations with your parents only if you want something from them. Otherwise, it just gets their hopes up for more.

8. Listen selectively to instructions from grownups. That way, you can always plead ignorance later.

9. Perform only the minimum you are asked to do, in order to keep expectations low.

10. Try not to agree with your parents' opinions too often. It sends the wrong message.

It used to take so little to excite my children. If I handed them iced cookies from the bakery, I was rewarded with beaming, ear-to-ear smiles. An extra half-hour of television time would result in squeals of joy and, "You're the best, Mom!" I miss being popular. These days, I could probably wake my teens with a surprise we're-going-to-Disney-World announcement, and they'd say, "Do we have to get up right now? Can we go later?" No matter what I tell them to do, how I phrase it, or when I impart any information or directions, my teenagers generally don't want to hear it. The bottom line is that they don't want to be directed by me at all—even if they desperately need my help, and we both know it. All this is a perfectly natural part of growing up. I understand that, but it still hurts my feelings.

The personification of this phase is perfectly captured in a scene from the movie *My Big Fat Greek Wedding*. The bride's aunt and mother are hatching a plan. The aunt says, "Tell me what to say, but don't tell me what to say." That's how teenagers feel all the time, I think. It absolutely wears me out.

I'm not a fan of the know-it-all teen or the I'm-too-cool-to-get-visibly-excited-about-anything teen. To combat such common pitfalls, frequent attitude adjustments are as necessary as teeth cleaning. There's no way around it. We have minor adjustments at least once a week around here.

One of my pet peeves that often provokes an attitude adjustment occurs when a teenager *tells* me what he or she is going to do as he or she heads out the door. Telling—rather than asking—skips right on over that pesky ask-for-permission step. I don't like that.

"Bye, Mom. I'm going to _____ with _____. See you later!"

"Would you like to rephrase that, sweetie?"

"Huh?"

That's when I give him or her *the look*. Every mom has *the look*. Words are unnecessary. *The look* speaks volumes. I can use it to control my children from all the way across the room. It's quite handy.

"Oh, *fine*, Mom. *May* I please do _____ with _____ tonight?"

A question is a horse of a different color, as far as I'm concerned. I'm not running a hotel here. It's my job to know where those people I gave birth to are at all times, which is tricky. They can be elusive. Sometimes, it's like trying to get the governor on the phone to stay an execution, or trying to spot the Loch Ness monster in the middle of his/her foggy lake.

I have even been known to pull off the side of the road if an immediate attitude adjustment is called for. On the way to a 6:30 a.m. baseball practice (which meant I was cooking breakfast at 5:45 on the first day of summer, like a farmer's wife on the prairie), my son complained so much in the car that I pulled off for a come-to-Jesus meeting that couldn't wait one more second.

"What exactly is your problem, son?" I asked.

"It's stupid to have practice this early! I'm in a bad mood because I had to get up on the first day of summer! What do you expect? Why did you have to get me up so early?" He asked this with a martyred air, as if it were somehow my fault.

I let his little tirade hang in the air for a few seconds and then took a deep breath to lay it on the line in terms my teenager would understand.

"Let me tell you exactly what I expect. You will be polite and respectful when you talk to me. I'll give you a pass on *friendly* this morning. It's a little early for friendly. *Polite* is going to happen, or we can sit here in this car all morning long."

"*Mom!* Start the car! I'm going to be late!" he bellowed, panicked.

"No way. You owe me an apology. Then I'll give you a chance to start over. That's the good thing about moms. You get unlimited chances to start over. That's good because you need a lot of chances."

"That's so stupid, Mom! You don't understand anything!"

"Do you want to play baseball, son?"

"What? Of course, I do! You know that!"

"Fine. This is part of it. I have no control over baseball. All I do is sign you up, write a huge check I can barely afford, wash your uniforms, and transport you, you ungrateful wretch. I assure you it is not convenient for me to take you to the school at this hour. I have two other children, a husband, and a job. Get it? You don't have to do this. In fact, it will be much easier for me if you don't.

It will be cheaper, too, and I can think of a lot of fun things to do with my free time other than sit in sweaty ballparks all season long. If you want to play, that's okay, too. I'll support you. However, I am not listening to another word of complaint. Practice is whenever the coach tells you to be there. I do not have one thing to do with it. Those coaches control my schedule, too, you know. My work and vacation days are held hostage all the time by football, basketball, and baseball coaches. I am not going to argue with you about this. If you want to do it, I'll make it happen for you. If you don't, quit. This isn't school. You have to go to school. You don't have to play sports. It's your choice. There will be early-morning practices, late-night practices, and homework to do at eleven o'clock—sometimes after you lose a game, when you are hot, tired, hungry, and in a bad mood. That's the way it goes. You know that. Make a decision right now. Suck it up and play, or don't. It's entirely your call. Either way, you will not talk to me like this again. Understand?"

"Yeah."

"What?"

"Yes, ma'am."

"And?"

"I apologize. I do want to play."

"Good deal. Now, what do you want for lunch when you get home?"

With teenagers, once it's over, it's over. There's no point in dwelling on past sins. Onward and upward.

Another stage most teenagers go through that occasionally requires some fine-tuning is the hermit crab phase. That's when teenagers hole up in their rooms like they're hiding out from the Mafia. The only way you know they're still breathing in there is because the music is usually turned up loud enough to rattle the windows and send tiny rivers of cracking plaster raining down from the ceiling. They emerge periodically like wild animals to forage for food in the kitchen and then scurry back into their rooms to talk for hours on end to their friends on cell phones or the computer. When guests—adults or teenagers—come over, we demand that the cave dwellers emerge to speak and engage in social interaction to keep up their people skills. But it doesn't last long. Adults aren't as interesting to teenagers as their own kind.

The hermit crab stage didn't last long around here, I'm relieved to say. My kids moved quickly from that phase to hanging out with their friends every single moment they aren't in school, participating in extracurricular activities, sleeping, or eating. If one of my teenagers ever accidentally arrives home one minute before his or her curfew, he or she will stand on the front stoop and talk to friends until time runs out. Coming in before one's curfew just isn't done in teenager world.

When family events roll around, I have to make sure to give my kids plenty of advance warning that their presence will be required. My people have to check with their people. You know how it is.

"Don't forget your grandfather's birthday lunch on Sunday!" I remind them a few days beforehand.

"We will all be eating together at 6 P.M., got it?" I shout as I hear the front door slam.

"You have to get a haircut this week—no excuses!" I begin with that one on Monday and hope that by Friday, the haircut has happened.

"I expect to see you at your sister's play on Tuesday!" I warn the boys in my house.

"Sure, sure, we haven't forgotten," they answer irritably. They always make me feel like a too-big-for-my-britches member of the White House staff who lobbies constantly to get on the president's appointment schedule, confident that this will eventually result in an ambassador's appointment to some small island in the South Pacific.

Parenting is the hardest job in the world. Period. The logistics are mind-boggling. Believe me when I tell you that it is not one bit of fun to be in charge of other people's dental hygiene, doctor visits, sports injury rehabilitation, clothing, money, schoolwork, and the thousand other things you have no idea you're signing up for when they hand you that nine-pound bundle at the hospital, roll you in a wheelchair to the front door, and tell you to toddle on home. I never in my life thought I would have to tell someone with bigger feet than my own, "You have to cut your toenails today."

There is no more humbling work on the face of the earth than being a mother. The chauffeuring services alone are enough to turn off most prospective parents. In addition to the work itself, which is hard enough, it's all uphill. Teenagers do not appreciate what their parents do until much, much later in life. They do not have a positive attitude or a pleasing disposition a lot of the time. Nobody who is doing a good job of it has an easy time raising teenagers. That's such a shame. It shouldn't be that way. It doesn't have to be that way. Sadly, it usually is that way.

Here's the punch line: it's all worth it. I'm telling the truth. That's how God gets you. Once you count those little fingers and toes, smell that newborn head, and feel the weight of that baby in your arms, you're hooked. No matter how hard the future is, you never regret having children. You love them no matter what. I don't know how that works, but it's true. I always tell my kids that even if they go to prison, I'll visit them and bring brownies. That doesn't mean I'll condone whatever crime sent them there. But I'll never stop loving them. Never. That doesn't mean I have to *like* the little suckers all the time, however. I don't. Parental love is fierce and illogical. I think it is the strongest force on earth. It trumps everything, thank God: mounds of laundry, sleepless nights, hard stadium seats, endless recitals, broken hearts, losing seasons, throw-up viruses, bad grades, poor choices, and everything else life throws at teenagers and their parents. In the end, when nothing else connects you to your teen, and you seem to be worlds apart, love remains. That's the saving grace.

THE NOT-SO-SWEET SOUNDS OF TEEN 'TUDE

1. "You don't understand anything!"

2. "It's not that big of a deal, Mom."

3. "I'll do it tomorrow."

4. "Nobody cares but you."

5. "It won't cost anything."

6. "I don't have any homework."

7. "Somebody must have stolen it."

8. "You can check me out. We're not doing anything in school today."

9. "I hate it/that/them/him/her!"

10. "Nobody writes thank-you notes anymore."

11. "There's nothing to eat in this house!"

12. "I turned it in for sure."

13. "I just found out about it."

14. "I need another check."

Do I Have to Pay for That?

To teenagers, money is an abstract concept. They can count money as skillfully as professional football bookies, of course. It's not about the math. The problem is that the sums don't mean much because there is no real-life context for them. Teenagers have no experience with agonizing decisions such as, "Should I pay the mortgage or the dentist's bill first?" Like sex and death, budgeting is something you have to experience firsthand to appreciate fully. Of course, most teenagers do not earn money or support themselves in any meaningful way. That is as it should be in our society. However, this means that teenagers understand money only theoretically. As every adult knows, it's a long way from Monopoly money to real-life cash.

In teenagers' minds, all the money the family brings in is split between two giant pots of dollar bills at the end of the rainbow.

One pot contains money that belongs to parents. Teens have a vague understanding that parents use this money to pay bills. Lord knows, they hear enough about that. Just ask your teenagers how often they've been told, "That's too expensive!" or "We can't afford that!"

How many times have you asked your teenager, "What did you do with the twenty I gave you yesterday?" My teens cannot seem to grasp the concept of change. I do not remember ever receiving any change from cash I have doled out to them, no matter how small or large the initial request was. They squirrel away my change in their back pockets like they expect to be asked to pay a poll tax at any moment. Teenagers bank (literally) on parents forgetting to ask for their change. My guess is that this is a good ploy. I bet it pays off more often than not. To combat the lack-of-change con game, I keep stacks of ones and fives like a purse-carrying drug dealer. I will give my child seven ones to go through a drive-through rather than the ten-spot most parents fork over without a second thought. I'm cheap. I have to be. We are on a tight budget. I'd love to be cavalier about small expenditures. Who wouldn't? I feel sure I'd be a genuinely delightful rich person. Unfortunately, I do not see that happening anytime soon.

My teens know that asking me for money while I am sitting at my desk paying bills is like poking a tiger with the barbecue tongs. Just interrupting me with a question is likely to bring on a tirade about the family budget, college tuition plans, federal income tax, the national debt, and the perils of late credit card payments. I can barely add and subtract without a calculator, so it might result in a balance-the-checkbook-for-Mama math assignment, too. No teenager in my house would make an amateur mistake like being in the same room when I am suffering through a bill-paying morning. When word leaks out that Mom is paying bills downstairs, my teenagers run like they're minors fleeing a bar with mai tais in their hot little hands during a police raid.

I feel fairly confident my teenagers understand that money earned by my husband and me is used to pay for such trifles as food, clothing, shelter, gas, insurance, orthodontist bills, and donations to the needy—luxuries like that. I've certainly explained it often enough. I am convinced they simply find such mundane matters beneath their interest. I get the feeling that they feel the family budget is not their problem. It is only when the budget affects them personally—their ability to go on spring break with friends or buy a prom dress that costs more than my entire maternity wardrobe, for example—that I can capture their interest in the ebb (trickle of incoming money) and flow (flood of outgoing money) of family finances. I think comedian Bill Cosby said it best when he told his teenagers, "I am rich. *You* have nothing."

The second pot of gold at the end of a teenager's rainbow holds money that is deemed to be the sole property of the teen. Unlike the money used by parents to pay bills, money teenagers hoard like greedy goblins is *theirs*. They have strong emotional ties to it. In their minds, it is their birthright, as if they are minor-league royals living on an allowance from the queen. (I understand that HRH Queen Elizabeth is famous for her thriftiness. I say, good for the old bag! She may be one of the richest women on the planet, but she has some serious upkeep with those castles.) Teens are positively miserly with their own money. Any contributions they make toward joint family presents or outings are reluctantly coughed up, at best. Teens ante-up only when driven to it by guilty consciences.

Considering how free and easy they are with *my* money, my kids are shockingly stingy with their own. They dribble out any money they have to pay one dollar at a time. On the rare occasions when I ask them for cash to tip the pizza delivery man, they scowl heavily and produce the money only after I sign an IOU promising prompt repayment with interest.

I swear teens are like bankers from hell. Their money is comprised of an allowance, birthday and holiday gifts, and the occasional payment for jobs performed during the summer, during Christmas break, and on a cash-poor-emergency-weekend-money-needed basis. To be clear: my teens have some jobs they must perform without any financial compensation at all. As members of a family, everyone does some chores for the common good, things like making beds, changing sheets, picking up a younger sibling from school or an activity, and taking out the trash—small jobs like that. And of course, any job performed while a teen is grounded at our house is, by definition, reparation for a crime or a shortfall in character. I don't pay a penny for jobs performed by prison inmates.

In short, in a teenager's mind, there is "my money" and "your money." "My money" belongs to the teen. "Your money" belongs to the parents. In a family, there is always some tension over the disbursement of discretionary income. Since parents work to earn every dollar they bring in to the household to support the little parasites they gave birth to, they assume—quite rightly, I think—that their discretion should determine how the few measly dollars left over after paying bills are spent. As you might expect, teenagers often disagree with those choices. To be fair, it's hard for anyone to get excited over a new water line that sucks up every extra penny in the family budget.

Teenagers always feel that they should spend their pocket money any way they see fit, without any supervision at all. If my daughter chooses to blow the equivalent of the GNP of a small nation on a pair of boots that will go out of style in six months, she feels strongly that I should be supportive of her idiotic choice. If my son chooses to spend his entire stash of Christmas cash on sunglasses he will wear to the pool one time (true story) before they are stolen, I am expected to keep my opinion about that lunacy to myself. As far as I am concerned, they might as well lean out the car window and scatter twenty-dollar bills on the highway. What a waste!

From a teenager's point of view, it all comes down to one question: "Am I paying for this, or are you?" Teens prefer that parents use funds from their own less interesting pot of gold for boring things like car insurance, medicine, and groceries. That leaves more money in the teens' pot of gold for eating out, going to movies and concerts, and otherwise entertaining themselves in the grand style to which they have become accustomed.

Speaking of that grand style, my husband and I realized a few years ago that we made one (okay, more than one, but I'm writing about only this one right now) big parenting mistake with our children. We created entitlement monsters. We didn't mean to do it. It was an accident—an oversight, really. Somehow, we gave our kids the impression that they reside in a very nice resort. In this resort, my husband and I are the support staff. The kids have no need to worry about expenses. They can just flash their key cards. They can order whatever they want in the resort restaurant. Cost is of no concern. They don't have to worry about lost or broken iPods, cell phones, or winter coats because all they need to do is report the loss to the staff, which will handle everything from there. Summer camp, braces, musical instruments, concert tickets, birthday presents for friends, sports equipment/uniforms, trips, tutorials, vacation money, trendy clothes, salon haircuts, acne products, concession food—the list goes on ad nauseam, or until we slam the till closed.

(This seems a good time for an aside: While compiling my pitiful list of tax deductions for my accountant this year, I learned for the first time that the IRS graciously allows parents to claim their children over the age of eighteen as dependents as long as they provide over half their support. That made me chuckle. How many eighteen-year-olds do you know who support themselves single-handedly? I can't think of a single one. A summer job or a part-time job is a big help, but it isn't enough to keep the average teenager in shower gel for a year. And while I'm on this soapbox, why isn't college tuition completely tax deductible? Isn't it in society's best interest to make it as easy as possible for parents to pay for college? Sometimes, I feel like the federal government has it in for me. It often makes it harder for me to do the right thing for my kids. I think the feds should be on my side! Don't you agree?)

We had a staff meeting at our house to discuss the monetary entitlement issues with regard to our guests/teenagers. We have no one to blame but ourselves. We're raising these kids. The buck stops here (pun intended). We're working our fat fannies off (I wish) night and day to make sure we get our kids to every school activity, in addition to their after-school extravaganzas. We pay for everything. We volunteer. We show up to support them. We stay up late to make sure they're safely home from their all-important social engagements. We get up early and jump on the treadmill again every single morning, no matter how tired we are.

My husband and I don't have a lazy bone in our bodies. How could we have raised children who feel perfectly comfortable with our working ourselves half to death to support their iTunes habits while they treat us like resort staff? I'll give you two examples. I could provide a hundred. I have actually vacuumed around a teen who did not even pause while watching a football game and texting at the same time to pick his feet up so I could clean underneath them. I have staggered into my house buried under a sea of grocery bags in full view of my children, who not only did not jump up to help but actively moaned and groaned when I yelled at them to get the heck up and unload the car. What kind of humans treat others like that? How could we have raised children who are that selfish? My husband and I are nice people. We really are.

Furthermore, my kids think they live in a *five-star* resort and that they are entitled to that level of housekeeping, kitchen, and car service. To add insult to injury, they think their eighteen-year stay at our very fine resort should be fully funded by the staff. That's right. Our kids think we should do all the work *and* pay for everything. You know what my teenagers believe is the sum total of their familial obligations? They think they should go to school and make good grades. Well, of course they should do that. That's the *minimum* requirement of guests here at Chez Thompson. But that's not all they should do. Parents are people, too, you know. We need a manifesto. I volunteer to write one.

Whoa.

After our two-person emergency staff meeting (which represents a very low employee-to-guest ratio for a five-star facility—no wonder I'm so tired), my husband and I decided to make some changes. We're always fine-tuning our parenting plan. There's nothing we relish more than a good ambush. Our family is a work in progress.

We decided to make a family announcement: "*We don't work for you anymore.*"

The announcement was not popular. The previous arrangement worked well for them, our teenagers explained. They saw no need for change.

"Tough tuna," we responded.

While I was glad my kids enjoyed their years lolling around the French Riviera, they were now going to experience resort services along the lines of those found in Third World border-town hostels. We, the hardworking staff, will continue to provide food, shelter, water, gas, electricity, and medical services on an as-needed basis. Everything else is to be determined.

"We're going to simplify things!" we announced. We explained how we needed to streamline our finances and become more budget-minded. It worked well for Southwest Airlines, and it could work for us, too. I even offered to throw in some free flight attendant humor. (I actually laughed out loud once when a Southwest attendant told passengers to "get the heck off now" at the end of a long flight I was on from Phoenix to Alabama.)

"This does not sound good," one of my sons muttered to his brother. He's our oldest child; he was suspicious right off. That boy is quick.

I am not good with money. Everyone knows it. When I get back home after selling my own books at speaking events, I open a big bag of M&Ms as an incentive before I figure out the sales taxes I have to pay. I feel inadequate teaching my teenagers about money. But like every other important life skill, I still have to teach it. None of us is born understanding how to budget, you know.

I decided to ask my British friend who is brilliant with money for help. She's raised two wonderful girls who were my kids' baby-sitters. They turned out well. (It's always good to see finished products that work well in the marketplace.) Her girls have had their own checking accounts since they were twelve years old. (I know it sounds impossible. I told you she's good.) My friend is a mean mama like me, so we're generally on the same page in reassuring one another about how right we are and how wrong the rest of the world is.

We set up a meeting, greased it with a glass of wine, and drew up a battle plan.

I said, "They can't do it. They *won't* do it."

She said, "Of course, they can. And yes, they will."

I protested louder. "I'm telling you, it won't work! My kids won't stick to the budget! They'll spend all their money up front! They'll bounce checks. I shudder to imagine what they'll do with debit cards. One of them might go to jail! It will end up being something else I have to police. You don't know my teenagers! They'll find a loophole, and I'll end up bailing them out!"

"You must stand firm," she said. "This *will* work."

When someone says that to you with a British accent, it sounds better than it would in regular American English. I decided to give it a try.

First, my husband and I had a financial summit on the porch. He was initially skeptical. He's never had the respect I do for the British. We fine-tuned my friend's plan, made it more boy-friendly, and beefed up the consequences section of the allowance contract.

Then we met with our kids. From their protests, you'd think we were dividing up postwar Europe at Yalta. To this day, my teens call the plan "the British Invasion."

Guess what? We've had some bumps (and one major crater) along the way, but the plan has worked overall. Giving them control over their own entertainment budgets cut down on a lot of arguing. No one has gone to jail. Yet. When their money is gone, it's gone—just like in real life.

"This stinks!" one of my kids said when he ran out of money.

"Well, yeah," I agreed. "I hate it, too. That happens to me all the time."

YOURS, MINE, AND OURS

1. "If I have to pay for it with my own money, I don't want it."

2. "My brother ate half of my fries, so he should pay half."

3. "Can I have my allowance a little early?"

4. "I didn't know when I spent the money that I would need it later."

5. "I'm eating at home before I go out. It's free."

6. "I didn't know they charged money for that."

7. "Wake up, Mom. It's the first of the month. Can I have my allowance?"

8. "I lost my wallet."

9. "If I use my money for that, I won't have any left!"

10. "Can I borrow some money? I need to buy you a Mother's Day present."

Curfew Conundrums

Curfews are a hot-button issue in any household with teenagers. Any major alteration, minor adjustment, temporary extension, inspired grace period, or unplanned deviation in a teenager's curfew—which has been intensely debated and reluctantly agreed upon by all parties concerned—requires delicate negotiation. If you are brave enough to enter this conversation, you better know how to defuse a bomb. If you have successfully bargained with market-stall vendors in foreign countries, you may have the skills needed to discuss curfews with teenagers. The key is defining reasonable restrictions. Bear in mind that the teenage definition of *reasonable* is "whenever I feel like coming home." If you have ever patrolled the halls of a maximum-security prison, the skills you've honed there will undoubtedly come in handy during your discussion. The Taser is optional. I personally believe that Tasering is beneath me. The day my kids are more afraid of a Taser than of me will be the day I surrender my parenting high ground.

Imagine a Middle Eastern peace summit where you and your offspring are invited to participate in negotiations. In this analogy, the parents are leaders of stable, well-respected, peaceful nations. They work well with fellow nations (other parents) in order to enforce agreed-upon curfews for the safety and benefit of all concerned. They genuinely want what is best for their people, the teenagers who live in their homes.

In direct contrast, teenagers are young, impetuous tyrants of small rogue nation-states. They are self-absorbed, unpredictable, and prone to tantrums and petty behavior. They are indifferent to the solvency of the family budget and happy to sacrifice long-term gains (money saved for college or family vacations) in exchange for short-term fun (money to pay for dinner and a movie tonight). If left unsupervised, teenagers will bankrupt their small fiefdoms in short order. They will stay up all night and sleep all day. They will eat nothing but junk food. Like their fellow tyrants in real life, if left unchecked, they will do only those things that give them pleasure. That means no schoolwork, no chores, and nothing for anyone else unless there is something in it for them. Teenagers believe that their actions should not be restricted in any way—certainly not by something as subjective and arbitrary as a curfew. Do these tyrants sound like anyone you know? I bet Kim Jong-il never had a curfew, and just look how he turned out.

The whole curfew discussion begins with the parties already divided into two extreme camps. One party takes the position that "curfews are stupid," designed primarily to inflict further suffering on an already oppressed people. (Gag.) The opposition party is equally passionate about its platform: "Curfews save lives." (Amen!)

For years and years of relatively smooth-sailing childhood, my kids followed my directives well. Life was good. If I said, "Let's go swimming!" they fled down the hall to pull on their swimsuits, shedding their clothes along the way. If I said, "So sorry, the mall is closed today," they didn't doubt my pronouncement for a moment—even if the parking lot was crammed full of holiday shoppers. They believed me, no matter what. That's the way God designed kids. It's very clever, when you think about it. I knew that if I shouted, "No!" or "Stop!" in an I-mean-business tone of voice, my children would respond immediately, no questions asked. It kept them safe on several occasions—when one more step would have sent my middle child into the marina, when my older son reached for a red-hot coal in the grill, when my daughter was just about to eat cat poop. God knew what he was doing when he built that listen-to-your-mama instinct right into their little brains.

I love how children look at your face for clues as to how they should react. Even when they hurt themselves, they check *your* face to see just how upset *they* should be. My first response was always, "You're okay!" with a big smile. It usually worked. I often saw moms rush over at the slightest skinned knee, and their kids reacted to every scrape as if it were an amputation. Kids read facial expressions well. It's one of the things that helps them live long enough to be teenagers. I think the last thing an angel tells a baby before sending her down to earth is, "Keep your eyes on the one with the breasts. She's your ticket to ride, okay?" I miss those times. I never thought I would when I was getting through each day hour by hour in a sleep-deprived fog, but I do. The grass is always greener, right?

When my children grew older, they began to question my omnipotence. This was perfectly normal for them and predictably unpleasant for me. I know that this is God's design, too, so that they can grow up to be independent people with minds of their own.

However, I'm not totally convinced God thought this part of the plan all the way through. I wish he'd checked with me first. I was quite fond of that blind obedience thing we had going on around here.

I liked being the most popular person on the planet when my kids were toddlers. If you asked my middle child, "Whom do you love best?" he always said, "Mom!" Now, he'd prefer that I wait in the car when we go somewhere together. One of my favorite things to do when my kids were babies was to walk down to the church nursery to pick them up after a service because they immediately abandoned whatever they were playing with and threw up their arms to be picked up as soon as they spotted my face. I can still see the smile curving around the edges of my younger son's pacifier. I loved that. It was the best feeling in the world. You can't tell me it isn't great to be loved so passionately that someone cries when you leave the room because it is.

Now, when I wake that same child in the morning by softly saying, "Morning, sweetie, it's time to get up," the first thing he does is groan at me. That is usually followed by a roll-over in bed, an arm pulling the covers over his head, and a curt, "*Okay, I'm up.*" I miss being popular. I admit it. Nothing in the world is better than going in to pick up a baby first thing in the morning or after naptime. Babies are always glad to see you. They are always in a good mood. Even if they are burning up with fever, they still greet you with a big, drooling grin. They always want to be kissed and cuddled, and they are up for pretty much anything if you can do it with one hand while they are parked on your hip.

I was good with babies. Teenagers—not so much. I don't get many hugs anymore. Any I do receive are inevitably instigated by me while they stand there like martyrs tied to a stake. My boys are significantly taller than I am. It's like hugging a tree trunk. Recently, when I was the rare recipient of a spontaneous hug from my seventeen-year-old, I got so excited I dropped the basket of chocolate-chip muffins in my hands. I was anxious to hug back while it was still on offer. It was totally worth the muffin loss.

My teenagers are ashamed to be seen with me. I'm just going to go ahead and say it. I don't know why! I try hard not to do anything that embarrasses them. I don't wear trendy clothes. I keep my remarks to a minimum when their friends are around. I voluntarily feed them and their friends and provide car service at all hours of the day and night. I love them with reckless abandon! How can they not like me? Other people like me. I have lots of friends. I do. I received my lowest popularity poll number the day I took a spill in the high-school parking lot. I went head over heels—a real tumble down a steep hill. I lifted my eyes to the hills from whence cometh my help just in time to see that my middle child had witnessed my unladylike wipeout. Two seconds later, I watched him laugh nervously, tuck his head, and run *toward* the school and *away* from me. That's right. He literally left me in the road to die. Well, okay, that's a slight exaggeration. I wasn't in danger of actually dying from anything except embarrassment, but that isn't the point! My feelings are still hurt. And yes, I plan to hold that against him until my dying day.

Teenagers want to talk about only the subjects of interest to them, and only when they are in the mood to vent. You can see how any discussion of curfews falls way, way down the list of topics of interest. Curfews cause friction (a nice school-counselor term for a big, ugly fight) between parents and teens. When pre-driving teens first get a taste of independence, they are free within certain parameters—a few blocks of the neighborhood, usually. It was a big deal around here when our kids were old enough to walk to the community pool, to the library, home from school, and to the candy shop or pizza joint. (Yeah, I really do live in a Mayberry-like community with great public schools and sidewalks, and yes, I know how lucky I am.) The first curfew was dinnertime or thereabouts—sometime before dark. In the next step toward independence, my kids met their friends in neighborhood restaurants to socialize and headed home about nine or ten. My fifteen-year-old is now six-foot-one and 175 pounds. I have cautioned him repeatedly about waiting until the last minute and then running home to make his curfew. It is only a matter of time before some little old lady spies him streaking through her front yard and calls the police.

Before I shed the last of the baby weight, however, my little terrors were driving themselves, and then the curfew discussions got dicey. When they added dating to that mix, things became really interesting. When my seventeen-year-old goes out on a Friday or Saturday night, the conversation runs something like this:

"Mom, I'm going over to So-and-so's house. Where's my blue button-down? Is it ironed?"

"Your shirt is in your closet. Would you like to rephrase that first part, son?"

"What? What do you mean? I'm late! I still need to shave!"

"Ma'am?" I prompt. "You meant *ma'am*, right?"

"*Ma'am?*" Sarcastic tone and a teenage eye roll here. The tone is civil, but barely.

I take a deep breath and give my kid a hard look over the top of my reading glasses. "Did you just ask me a question? If you did, I missed it," I say in my calmest, best passive-aggressive mama voice.

This is about the time in the dialogue for a big, dramatic sigh from my teenager. "*Fine.* Mom, *may* I go to So-and-so's house tonight?"

"Sure. Who's going to be there?"

"I don't know! Just some guys!"

"Which guys? Is So-and-so"—a known troublemaker—"going to be there? Are the parents going to be home?"

"I don't know! Why are you asking me all these questions? You're like the Gestapo!"

"I need that information if you want to go, please. Any girls going, too?"

"What difference does that make? It's not a dating thing! We're just hanging out."

"I think that's great, but I still need to know those things before you leave. Text and find out, please."

"Why do you always have to make such a big deal out of everything, Mom? Nobody else's parents do. You make me feel like the biggest geek in America."

"Sorry. I like geeks. They usually do rather well when they grow up. Some of the most successful people in history started out as geeks and ended up changing the world. Bill Gates, for example. Remember that. You should be nice to geeks. One day, you'll be glad you were."

"Why do you always start these weird conversations, Mom? I don't care about geeks! I just want to go to So-and-so's house, and you turn it into a parenting moment. Can I go now?"

"Absolutely. Quick review: what time is your curfew?"

"Eleven. You don't have to tell me every time. I'm not an idiot. It's not like I'm going to forget, since I'll be the first one who has to leave. All my friends have later curfews than I do. Jack doesn't even have a curfew."

"You know perfectly well that's because Jack doesn't have any parenting at all. Nobody cares whether Jack comes home at night or not. Think about that for a minute. And tell him he can spend the night here if he wants to."

"'kay."

"This does not mean that you call me at eleven to tell me you are on your way. It does not mean eleven-fifteen. It means that you are in this house where I can see you, smell your breath, and ask about your evening when the clock strikes eleven, Cinderella. Got it?"

"Cinderella's curfew was *twelve*, but yes, ma'am, I got it. Can I go now?"

"That means you leave at quarter 'til. Understand? I do not want you to wait until the last minute and then have to rush home. It's not worth it. Leave yourself plenty of time. All kinds of stupid, drunk people are out there driving. And wear your seatbelt, okay?"

"Okay. I always wear my seatbelt. You know that."

"I do know that, but I'm afraid that the one time I don't remind you will be the time you forget."

"You know you're a little bit weird, don't you, Mom?"

"I do, actually. Have fun, son. Love you."

"Loveyoutoobye."

Each year of high school, my kids get little-bit-later curfews. There is a direct correlation between my kids' curfews and the dark circles under my eyes. I thought that when my children finally slept through the night as babies, I was never going to have to stay up all night again. Boy, was I ever naïve. Once you have teenagers, it's back to life as a sleep-deprived zombie. They stay out late and come home excited to tell you all the latest gossip. You stay awake or doze in bed or on the sofa so that you can examine their faces and check for damage to body, heart, or soul when they come in. And then, while they sleep late the next morning, you get up to go to work or do the regular errand-running of life. Once that pregnancy test comes back positive, you can pretty much kiss eight hours a night goodbye. (As an interesting aside, I just read that lack of sleep causes weight gain—like I needed another thing to be mad at teenagers about.)

Of course, if you set a curfew, you know what is going to happen, don't you? It's as inevitable as teenage acne. Somebody is going to feel compelled to break that curfew, which results in consequences—a whole different chapter I'll get to in a minute. We have a standard rule here for minor infractions: every minute that you are late costs you that amount of time the next night out. It's simple and easy to calculate. For major violations, I've been known to respond more creatively. The more overdue the kid is, the longer I've had to worry and stew, and the more stringent my responses become.

I'm not the only clock-watching mama in the world either. I have several mean-mama friends. I am comforted by that. There is strength in numbers, you know. In fact, one of my friends is even more suspicious than I am about what our kids are up to. I was a goody-goody in high school. She was not. Over the years, she has solved teenage crimes that would have baffled me. She's clever like that. She once told me that she thought she could commit the perfect crime. She was at least half-serious. She meant the planning, I think. She's not big on blood. She's creative, like me. You don't want to blow off your curfew with creative mean mamas like us. We're going to make you suffer for every single one of those minutes we spend walking the floor and worrying about the ETA of your little butt.

SORRY I'M LATE

1. "I was just about to come home when you called/texted me."

2. "I got lost because everything looks different at night."

3. "I didn't know you were that serious about it."

4. "I had to drive a friend home, and his mom had brownies."

5. "I was already going to be late, so I didn't think it mattered how late."

6. "I had to pick up my backpack/uniform/ wallet/homework in my friend's car. You always tell me to bring everything home."

7. "I had to stop for gas. Do you want me to run out of gas?"

8. "I thought I'd get an extra hour because of the time change."

9. "I figured you'd be asleep. Other parents go to bed. Why do you wait up?"

10. "I was the first one to leave the party, so I can't be late."

11. "I gave a girl a ride home so she'd be safe. I was being a gentleman."

12. "I was having too much fun to leave."

13. "I was with a friend who has a later curfew."

14. "I was hoping you wouldn't notice. It was worth a shot."

15. "I thought since I made all As on my report card, you'd be okay with it."

16. "Since you and Dad were going out for dinner, I didn't think you'd find out."

17. "I know I'm late, but it was totally worth it."

Have You Considered the Consequences?

pparently, this is the chapter all my friends look forward to reading most in this book, mainly because they're a bunch of ghouls who can't wait to see what goes down in our house when our teenagers get in trouble. That's what reality television has done to this country. We all want to see the down-and-dirty in other people's lives to make sure we're not the *worst* parents out there. We're all looking for reassurance. "At least my kid isn't in prison or rehab," we say to one another. That bar is pretty darn low for parents in the age of television reality shows, isn't it?

Most of us parents want to compare our "family consequence plan" (a new-school phrase to describe what happens when our kids get in trouble) to other parents' plans. "I told my daughter she better never speak to me like that again or I'll pop her right in the kisser," I heard from a girlfriend of mine who is about four and a half feet tall, weighs about a hundred pounds after Thanksgiving dinner, and is about as intimidating as a chipmunk in pin curls. I think we're all just hoping to stumble upon a brilliantly clever punishment that will work miracles in our own households. My advice: don't hold your breath.

If that's why you're reading, well, I want you to know that I feel your pain, and best of luck to you. I'm not an expert on parenting, you know. You could probably get sued for adopting some of my suggestions. I'm doing the best I can. I call living with teenagers *triage parenting*. My worst days are the inspiration for (sub)urban legend. My best days make me feel like we might all live through this and come out on the other side still speaking to one another. Personally, I'm not that fascinated by other people's punishments, although I did once tour a wing in a museum devoted to the display of medieval torture devices, so maybe I'm more of a voyeur than I'd like to admit.

So, do you want to know just how ugly punishment can get around here? I guess it's time for full disclosure. The answer is: very, very ugly.

At some point along the way, with one child or another, my husband and I have tried it all. Some things have worked like a charm. Others haven't. Punishments that worked well for our friends' kids have had no impact on ours at all. What motivates one of our kids does not necessarily work well with the other two. We've screamed and yelled. We've cried and fussed. We've talked, discussed, argued, nagged, and whined. We've thrown things. We've occasionally slammed doors and stomped off in fits of temper. We've taken away treats and privileges like car keys, video games, and concert tickets. We've added chores, too—cleaning assignments, yard work, and anything else that requires lots of time and old-fashioned elbow grease. Our kids are strong and healthy. They do good work when they are properly motivated. For example, I say, "I don't care how long this job takes you, but you can't leave the house until it's done to my satisfaction." Free tip: you should always attach a mandatory parental inspection clause when you hand out a punishment. Upon completion of any job your teenagers do as reparation, the work has to pass muster. I learned this the hard way. Otherwise, they do the least they can get away with. Make your expectations crystal-clear at the outset. If your teenagers have just been saddled with punishments that wreck their plans for a fun weekend, their attitude is already in the toilet. Remember: generally speaking, teenagers take no pride in the work they do for you.

Like most of you, we've also dabbled in the reward system. We've offered prizes like it's Bingo night on the reservation. We've dangled extended curfews, free movie tickets, and special outings with friends.

We never get "crafty" with our punishments or rewards, although I know some parents who enjoy that. I have never created posters, awarded stickers, or heated up the glue gun to make a visual aid. That's a little too involved for our household. We're busy people and way too tired for all that business. In a fit of temper one day, I did start a tally system on a paper towel and taped it to the refrigerator with a piece of duct tape. (We love duct tape around here. Anything can be fixed with duct tape. Right now, duct tape is the only thing holding one of the shelves in my refrigerator in place. It's been there for years. Unless all my readers buy a lot of books, it's going to be there for a few more. We also have a bit of decorative duct tape trim on our icemaker. All of our appliances are aging beauties, real *Architectural Digest* material.) On that paper towel, I wrote my kids' names in big, angry caps with a black Sharpie. For a few weeks, I put a hash mark by each kid's name every time I had to pick up a wet towel from their bedroom floors or fish out a dirty glass from underneath their beds. At the end of the month, my plan was to subtract a dollar from each kid's allowance for every dirty towel or glass I had to pick up. The way I looked at it, they could either clean up after themselves like civilized human beings or pay me to do it. That consequence program lasted a couple of weeks until it petered out, as do so many of my rage-inspired plans.

Like all parents, my husband and I want our children to learn that every single thing they do has a consequence—for good or for ill. We want our kids to consider the costs of their actions—to pause for a moment before doing something stupid and weigh the benefits of what they want to do in the short term against the potential consequences in the long run. I think that such a pause is sometimes long enough to bring them to their senses. One of my teenagers might think, for example, *If I jump off Chimney Rock and my mom sees a picture of it on Facebook, she might not let me go back to the lake with my friends again all summer.*

It's a lot like training a puppy. It takes positive and negative reinforcements to safely shepherd teenagers to adulthood. You have to find the perfect combination. I know an adult whose parents refused to allow him to watch the news on television as a punishment when he was in his teens. That was the perfect button to push to get what they wanted. My teenagers do not care if war has broken out on the East Coast, as long as it doesn't mess up their plans for the weekend. But taking away their cell phones causes them to scream like someone being chased in a slasher movie.

In case you are still wondering (or hoping), I am not one of those gentle, soft-spoken, sweet mamas who always sees the good in her children no matter what they do wrong or what they are accused of doing wrong. (If you've read my other three books, this will not surprise you. I write nonfiction. All my material comes from my life. It's free and plentiful, since God gives me lots of character-building lessons. But it can also be humbling and embarrassing—nationwide.) My children know that if they get in trouble, they better have the DNA evidence to back up any pleas of innocence. We do not begin with a presumption of innocence around here. They have to be able to prove they're *not* guilty. No jury of our teenagers' peers is waiting to hear testimony and weigh the evidence. I'm a firing squad kind of judge, and I am often quick to line people up against the wall. My husband is a real judge. He tends to think carefully before he speaks. My kids aren't nearly as afraid of him as they are of me. I'm much more likely to shoot first and ask questions later.

My kids will tell you I'm a mean mama. I'm not ashamed of that reputation anymore. But my kids also claim I enjoy being a mean mama. Now, that's just not true. It hurts my feelings that they think so. I'd much rather be one of those sweet mamas who speaks in a soft voice and gets her children to behave appropriately by inspiring them to do the right thing with little songs and heart-shaped cookies. That mama never screams until she is hoarse (did that today), grabs a handful of her foot-taller son's shirt to bring him down to eye level so she can fuss some more (a common occurrence), or runs behind a teenager's car with a broom (which happened only one time—let's just say he had it coming and leave it at that).

Who wouldn't rather be a sweet mama? There's no dignity in

being a mean mama. My style of parenting is no Norman Rockwell painting. I'm not checking my mailbox for my Mother of the Year award either. My point is that parenting isn't about me. It's about doing what I think is best for my children. Does that mean I'm right about everything? Of course not. (This is a real shame. My least favorite person's fault for things to be is mine.) Does it mean I never have to apologize to my offspring? No again. I apologize and start anew at least once a week.

The reality is that I haven't found sweet mamas to be nearly as effective as mean mamas. So, while I'm not particularly proud of being mean, I am proud of the results I get. My kids are turning out rather nicely, thank you very much. I could brag here, but I'll restrain myself. I do not want to be one of those mamas. Sure, some of my kids' successes are the product of good genetic material. Also, my kids were lucky enough to be born to parents who love one another and them. We work to support them every day of their expensive little lives. But the secret ingredient to their success is that they have a mean mama. I can't stress that enough. It pays to be clever, sneaky, quick thinking, and adaptable, but most of all, you have to have a dab of mean and nasty, like the Grinch. I can't say it any plainer than that.

My husband and I often refer to our oldest child as "the Experiment." He's our first attempt at parenting. We're learning as we go along. We've made some mistakes. We admit that. We have some regrets. We've committed sins of omission and commission. We try to do a little bit better with each child who comes along. I think if we have about fifty more, we'll be prepared to parent the last five like true professionals.

One of my biggest disappointments in parenting is that each of our three kids is different. It makes me feel a little bit cheated.

I've talked to other parents, and this is true in their families, too. Just when I figure out the best way to teach a life lesson or to handle a problem, the next kid presents totally different challenges. The perfect punishment for one kid doesn't even faze another. It sure would be helpful if there were an instruction manual or a special-order form that came with each delivery. I can imagine it now: "Congratulations, new mama! It looks like you've got the new-baby math brain with just a smidgen of musical talent. You must be so proud! You and your husband enjoy that model, you hear? Please read the fine print before having sex. We do not accept returns or exchanges."

In many ways, parenting any teenager is one big experiment. You go into it with certain theories. You have hopes and dreams. It's the biggest investment of your life, emotionally and financially. Each decision is potentially life altering. As a parent, you are responsible for growing a person. If you stop and think about that for a minute, it will bring you to your knees. I guarantee it.

You can't raise a teenager without spending way more time than you ever thought you would discussing consequences, punishments, reparations, and occasionally prison time. Whatever you call punishment at your house, it amounts to the same thing. If you make a rule, your kid is going to break it at some point along the way, if only to test the limits of your resolve. Then you have to decide what you want to do about that.

Wide-ranging options are available—a whole world of possible repercussions for every infraction, many more than I have talked about in this chapter. And somebody thinks of something new every day. Sadly, there is an ever-expanding world of trouble your kids can get into. Sometimes, it's just a matter of rule breaking. Other times, you're dealing with basic morality, right and wrong, and the true nature of temptation. These days, you need a law degree and a medical license to raise children. Who knew? It is also helpful if you can channel Plato and some of his buddies. Parenting requires you to delve into meaty issues. In many ways, rearing teenagers is an ongoing case study in ethics and philosophy.

Over the years, I have received more free advice about discipline than any other aspect of parenting. This surprises me. Browse the parenting section in your local bookstore. You'll be amazed by what you find. Apparently, most parents have at least one moment when they wonder if their teenager is going to grow up to be a serial killer. The main thing to remember is that teenagers screw up and make bad choices, no matter what you say, how many warnings you give, and what kind of example you set.

Parents differ in how they respond. One size does not fit all. You have to find what works for your kid and your family. The important things are to find the consequence that will work and to impose it consistently and as often as necessary to get the result you want: a happy, responsible, self-supporting adult who doesn't live in your basement when he or she grows up.

As far as I can tell, there's no magic recipe. It's a complicated mixture of carrots and sticks. You want to motivate and inspire like a sweet mama does, but you also want to come down like a ton of bricks on issues regarding safety, unkindness, laziness, and sheer cussedness. I wish I could tell you what to do. If I ever figure it all out, I'll get a memo out ASAP. I can tell you only what has worked for me, the mean mama.

When kids are still in single digits, consequences are relatively easy to apply. You can redirect, distract, or remove the temptation or the kid from the situation. Consequences are usually immediate, which is how it should be. Yesterday is ancient history to a toddler. Little kids live in environments controlled by parents. I loved parenting my kids at that age. I'm a big fan of control. Time-out worked for me. I have friends who ask, "How did you make them stay in time-out?" I don't know how to answer that. My kids never got up until I told them they could. I found it easy to manage toddlers. They're not hard to outsmart. I'm a resourceful woman. Also, little kids crave their parents' approval. They actively seek to please. Don't you love that about them? I do.

Teenagers are another matter entirely. It's a quick ride from Play-Doh to prom night. Suddenly, you're there. Teaching teenagers the consequences of their actions is like going straight from peewee football to the NFL draft with no stops in between. You have to hang tough and be ready to hit whatever comes over the plate. You have to field whatever comes at you. (I don't know what's with all the sports metaphors. They just feel right.)

Teenagers have quick reflexes and little to lose. They think fast on their feet. They're clever, and they were born technologically savvy. The best you can do is try to keep up. They can text with their cell phones in their pockets or under the table while you are talking to them about something else entirely. The kids you love more than your next breath will lie to your face with the audacity of antique dealers. They aren't inherently bad deep down inside— way deep down. It's just that they are wholly, completely, and totally absorbed in themselves. They want to do what they want to do, whether or not it is a good idea, whether or not they could get killed doing it, and whether or not the timing is right. The fact that they aim to please only themselves means that, quite often, what they want to do runs right smack into what you told them not to do. That's when things get sticky. They have to *choose* to do the right thing.

At our house, we are all about choices. "You always have a choice," I tell my kids. "If someone holds a gun to your head, you have a choice." The problem is that the choices stink. You can do what the gunman wants, or you can risk getting shot. No matter how much I talk about alcohol, drugs, sex, and other dangers, my teenagers ultimately have to decide for themselves how they are going to behave. The challenge for me is to convince them to choose wisely. "When you make a choice," I tell my kids, "you better be able to live with the consequences—in the big world and at home." It's a toss-up whom they fear more: me or God Almighty. "You always have to pay the piper," I remind them. With regard to sex, for example, I say, "Please don't allow ten minutes of fun result in eighteen years of child rearing. Once you have a child, that kid's needs become more important than yours. Got it?" You can't be vague with teenagers. You have to lay it on the line and hope they pick up what you put down.

Disciplining teenagers requires subtlety and creativity. You have to find a way to get them where it hurts without actually hurting them. I've found one of the most vulnerable areas on a teenager is the plug-in soft spot. My teenagers are attached to their cell phones, iPods, computers, and televisions with umbilical cords. One of the fastest ways to get their attention is to cut that cord. I promise you one thing: if you do this, your teenagers will pay attention to you. They may yell like they're being hacked to death with machetes, but they will hear what you have to say. Remind them that Mama giveth and Mama taketh away. It's all about finding the balance between rewards and consequences. It's a delicate dance.

Like most families, our run-of-the-mill, go-to consequence is grounding. In a nutshell, that means the teenager is restricted to the home front for whatever time period we designate. The teenager goes to school and whatever activity or event other people depend upon him or her for (why punish the whole baseball team because my kid misbehaved?), but that's all. His or her social life comes to a grinding halt. Sometimes, the kid gets to keep phone, television, or computer privileges, sometimes not. It depends on the nature and the magnitude of the crime. Was there premeditation? Was actual malice involved, or was it just a bonehead, spur-of-the-moment impulse? Was it a have-you-lost-your-mind choice or merely a what-were-you-thinking transgression?

The downside for the rest of the family is that the gloomy, bad-tempered, grounded teen is confined to the house—where everyone lives. On more than one occasion, a grounded teen in our home has added time to his or her sentence by behaving poorly while still under house arrest. It happens. Some monkeys learn faster than others.

Unlike most mamas, I do not allow grounded teenagers to lounge around. In my view, whatever the teen has done to result in a consequence of significance has caused harm to the family as a whole. The peace of the home has been disrupted—usually by screaming, at the very least. As a consequence, that teenager owes reparation to the family. In other words, the teen has some making up to do. My kids are assigned jobs when they are grounded. I'm not talking make-work either. I mean real work. We live in an old house. Something always needs work.

We have three children and two parents in our family. Every day, more work needs to be done than two parents can possibly do, no matter what time we get up in the morning (while the teenagers who kept us up all night sleep in). Therefore, I always have a to-do list on my desk. On that list are small jobs and big jobs, dirty jobs and clean(ing) jobs, outside work and inside work, mindless tasks and you-must-be-smart-to-handle-this jobs. Every second that the grounded teen is not eating, sleeping, or going to school is time that can be spent working and improving the world around them. If I can't think of anything appropriate (hasn't ever happened and never will), I'll farm my kids out to elderly neighbors like indentured servants. We're all about giving back to the community.

My kids have frequently been sentenced to spend the day polishing silver. I am especially quick to assign this punishment if we have a dinner party coming up soon. My kids have learned to be especially well behaved the day before a party. You'd be amazed how well those slim adolescent fingers can get into crevices with an old toothbrush to polish antique filigree. It's good for them to learn a new life skill, silver polishing, while serving a sentence for misbehaving. I love to double-dip. It is twice as satisfying. The result: clean silver and a repentant, silver-savvy teen. It's win-win.

Another obvious choice for punishment is yard work. This is particularly helpful if your teen is vocal about how unfairly he or she believes the imposed consequence is. If he's composing a letter to The Hague accusing you of crimes against humanity, tell him to take it outside. In the great outdoors, he can vent to the earth and sky to his heart's content. It's a cleansing exercise. Let him get it all out of his system while digging a hole for your new gardenia bush. You don't have to listen.

My kids can mow grass, plant flowers, trim borders, fertilize, and use the weed whacker and the blower. It is helpful to have a big job like yard work in your back pocket in case all the kids in your house misbehave at once or in the event they were all in on the same crime. If you want to make an especially memorable experience, I suggest the removal of a large bush or small tree. They're not easy to dig up. It's a dirty, sweaty job, even for an adult. It's particularly daunting if the shovel is taller than the kid holding it. Keep a list of jobs stored in your head. You never know when a teenager will screw up next. You might as well get something good out of it.

When one of my teens snuck out of the house using his bedroom window after coming in for his curfew on time, the sneak, I was shocked and furious, but a fitting punishment popped almost instantly to my mind, as if it had been planted there by God himself. I explained that since my teen was so familiar with the workings of the window and screen, he could put that knowledge to good use the next weekend by removing all the screens and washing all the windows in our home. I thought the punishment fit the crime in a tidy manner. It's nice when there's an ironic theme to the grounding. I do love a clever consequence.

Another time, my son's consequence was to spring-clean the porch—a big job, since it was the first cleanup after winter. It was easily a five-hour punishment. The pollen was so thick that the floor looked yellow. All of the furniture had to be removed from the porch, washed, and later returned. The cushions and pillows had to be cleaned. The walls had to be swept of cobwebs and washed. It was a filthy job. After issuing specific instructions and providing the cleaning equipment, I went about my day, confident that justice was being done and pleased that I'd also get a clean porch out of the deal.

After an hour or two, I heard my son talking to the neighbor who lives next door. I like my neighbor. He's a young doctor. He has two baby girls. Unfortunately, I think he's just a heartbeat away from calling the authorities to report us for child abuse. When he sees my kids working, he looks visibly appalled. *Just you wait*, I always think to myself.

"Hey," he said to my son, tentatively.

"Hey," my son answered as he tied a white T-shirt around his nose and mouth to keep the pollen out. I had heard him sneezing nonstop for over an hour. About sixty used tissues were wadded up on the swing, where he had thrown them in between swipes he was making with the mop. (This kid has the strongest work ethic of my three. He's big, muscular, and strong like only high-school athletes in the peak of condition can be. I always get better results when he's the one in trouble. The boy does great work.)

"Son, are you having an allergy attack?" my neighbor asked, the picture of a concerned physician. "I have some Claritin if you need it."

"No, sir, I'm okay," my son said.

My neighbor couldn't stand it. He had to know.

"Do you just like helping your parents out, or what? That's a big job you've got there," he pointed out—trying, I suppose, to gauge whether he should make an anonymous call to DHR or just go ahead and dial 911 and let the police sort it out.

Time to intervene, I thought.

I started walking toward the porch. I felt a little bad about the pollen. I knew one of my kids was really allergic, but I'd forgotten which one. I might have crossed a line there. Ideally, none of my punishments is designed to send any kid to the emergency room.

Before I opened the door, I heard my son's response: "Oh, no, sir, I don't like cleaning. This is a *consequence.*"

Well. What a good boy! I couldn't have said it better myself. You have to love a kid who responds like that. Lord knows, I do.

The next consequence I impose will be Christmas card labels. My current list is a big, fat mess. It will take many painful hours to organize. My kids have better computer skills than I do. The next time somebody gets in trouble, he or she is going to spend the weekend working on Christmas card labels. As a bonus, it will be a good reminder of how much we value our many, many extended family members. As my child sorts through the names and addresses of distant relatives, we'll review the whole family history together.

Doesn't that sound like fun?

CHOICES, CHOICES, CHOICES

1. "My brother/sister did the exact same thing, and he/she didn't get in trouble at all!"

2. "You should see what other kids do! I'm an angel compared to some of my friends!"

3. "You can't ground me until I'm thirty! That's ridiculous!"

4. "You should just trust me!"

5. "Just because other kids were drinking doesn't mean I was!"

6. "You can't be mad at me because of what someone else posts on my Facebook wall!"

7. "When I have kids, I'm going to let them do/pick/wear/go wherever/whatever they want!"

8. "You're totally overreacting! Nobody got hurt. This punishment isn't fair!"

9. "I didn't do anything wrong!"

10. "It wasn't even my fault!"

11. "Nobody else's mom grounded them!"

Where Did You Get That Idea?

One of the hardest things about parenting teenagers is: other people. They make my job more difficult than it has to be. I hate that. My teenagers' friends, other kids' parents, older siblings, cousins, grandparents, even actors, rock stars, musicians, and models—every person and her hair stylist has an opinion on the best way to parent teenagers.

It's like squirting lighter fluid on the grill when one of my teenagers says something like, "There's no reason we can't go to that concert at the beach by ourselves! So-and-so's dad says we're plenty old enough!"

In a sarcastic aside to my husband, I reply, "I understand why he wants the boys to go alone. He will be way too busy committing adultery that weekend to take the boys to that concert like he promised."

I have no problem with my kid's friend. However, I'm not a member of his father's fan club and never will be. The premise of this chapter is: if your friend jumped off a bridge, would you do it, too? Sure, it's a cliché, but that expression is still as true today as it was the day it was coined. The times may be a-changin', as Dylan suggested fifty years ago, but people are the same piece of work they've always been.

Have you noticed that nowadays more people than ever feel free to weigh in with their entirely unsolicited opinions on how to handle kids they didn't give birth to? I'm convinced it makes them feel virtuous to boss the rest of us around. News flash: when I need an opinion about how to parent my teenagers, I'll ask people I love and respect. I've certainly sobbed into my margarita with my close friends about the stress of rearing teenagers in today's complicated world. Sometimes, we all need a comrade in arms (another parent) to listen to our tales of woe. Usually, what I need most is shoring up. I need my friends to tell me to hang tough, to remind me that parenting is not a popularity contest, and to reassure me that I'm doing the right thing even if I feel like (and am beginning to look remarkably like) the Wicked Witch of the West.

When I hear pop stars spout off glib parenting advice on television, it makes me want to throw things at the screen. Sometimes, I do that almost-snorting thing with my nose that embarrasses my kids. (Of course, almost anything I do, like singing in church or breathing too loudly when their friends are around, embarrasses them.) Why in the world should I care about how Madonna parents her teenage daughter? We are not acquainted. I don't know what she's like in real life; she may be the soul of discretion, but some of the things I've seen her do and heard her say in front of God and everybody make me wonder. Maybe she lives up to her name in private. How would I know? What difference does it make if my kid's friend has never had a curfew in his life? Who cares if the neighbor's kid raises free-range chickens in his backyard? In what way is evidence from other people's lives and choices supposed to be persuasive to me about how to parent my own kids, except perhaps as a cautionary tale? I don't get it. Truly.

Think it is just kids who are influenced by the in-crowd? I have two words for you: *bottled water*. Water is free from the tap in the kitchen. Otherwise sane adults buy bottled water (with no greater purity standards than the water in the bathroom toilet) in fancy bottles with inflated price stickers. Talk about a fast one . . . I never thought Americans would fall for that. Of course, I never thought women would voluntarily pierce their tongues or tattoo their backsides either. Even food goes through popularity crazes. Heirloom tomatoes and goat cheese were all the rage for a while. Now, it's microbrewed beer and organic vegetables. Just imagine: teenagers are even more vulnerable than adults to whatever the cool crowd says is "in." We're all frail mortals. Will Shakespeare had us pegged a long, long time ago. Nothing much has changed since then.

I tell my children exactly what free advice is worth. I remind them to always consider the source. That's true for Internet research for high-school research papers and for big decision making about where they want to go to college, whom they should marry, and what they want to be when they grow up.

You know who always has parenting advice ready to serve up to unsuspecting members of the public? I bet you guessed this one: people who don't have children. They are always quick with the if-he/she-were-my-kid editorials. Yeah, yeah, right. They have some nerve, in my opinion.

I have a friend who called the bluff of some free-advice bums when he boarded an airplane for the first time with his three-year-old daughter. She began screaming for a favorite stuffed animal that was, sadly, safely stowed in checked baggage. No way was the toy making an appearance. He explained the situation patiently and logically to his daughter. The three-year-old didn't care for his explanation. In fact, the screaming escalated. My friend began to sweat. We can all identify with that. Who hasn't felt the pressure of being trapped in a public place with a child too young to be embarrassed?

He took note of the disapproving looks and snarky comments from passengers trapped in the surrounding seats. When the complaints of disapproving villagers rose to a fever pitch, my friend stood, turned his back on his red-faced, screaming daughter, and addressed the passengers as a group: "Okay, people, I'm really sorry about this. She's driving me crazy, too. I don't know anything else to do. I'm out of ideas. The floor is now open to suggestions. Short of hitting her or drugging her, I'll try anything you suggest."

Well, that shut them up. He let those words resonate in the cabin. Then he made eye contact with anyone brave enough to meet his gaze. Of course, none of those know-it-alls knew what to do either. However, they were highly motivated to come up with an it-takes-a-village solution because the prospect of a screaming three-year-old on a transatlantic flight was not a happy one for anyone. Finally, a woman opened her purse and offered her grandchild's book as a distraction. Another passenger came up with two crayons and a notebook. A young student offered a game on his iPad (and saw his self-sacrifice rewarded with a round of applause). Slowly, the tension level returned to normal in-flight misery. I think my friend did rather well, all things considered. Sometimes, there are no easy answers, and nobody knows it all, no matter how much smack they talk.

Some people just can't help sticking their noses in other people's business. They always think they know what other parents should do. Of course, their own kids are usually bullies, shoplifters, porn addicts, or compulsive gamblers. It is much more fun to look at other people's problems and see easy solutions.

"Why doesn't she kick her thirty-year-old pot-head son out of her guest room and make him get a job?" That's a real common scenario.

"If she didn't always bail that girl out, she'd learn a lesson!" We all know helicopter parents.

"I can't believe she lets her child talk to her like that!" I'm guilty of self-righteousness on this one. I've been tempted to jerk up a child I didn't give birth to after hearing him talk to his mother, my friend, like she is an idiot. It's one of my pet peeves. I have a very low threshold for this particular sin.

When someone shines a spotlight on our own issues, we always have reasons why our situation is "different." We are quick to explain why a suggestion won't work for us. Sometimes, it really does help to get another perspective from a friend who knows you and your teenager. You have to feel comfortable baring your soul or venting your spleen to that person. This confidante must be able to resist the urge to share the story of your teenager's mistakes all over town. You must have faith in your friend's counsel. Otherwise, there is no chance you will take her advice. If you choose to confide in a friend whose children are high-school dropouts, the problem may not be your teenager. It may be you. You may not have good sense yourself. It happens.

Bottom line: when my kids idolize friends or relatives who make bad choices, it makes my job so much harder. Isn't parenting challenging enough without people deliberately trying to sabotage you? I bet you have some friends or relatives like this in your own life. It's as common as shower curtain mildew. With friends and relatives mucking things up, who has time to worry about interference from famous people you don't even know? And have you seen some of the reality shows on television, by the way? Whose reality would that be? I am proud to say that I don't know anyone like those people on TV.

Before my kids were teenagers, other people's opinions didn't matter much. Their words were just white noise in the background of our lives. No way could they rock our little world. To toddlers, Mama knows everything. She's always right. If she needs backup, there's always Dad. If I said, "Try this—it's delicious," my children's mouths would open like baby birds'.

My three children had absolute faith in me. I had all the answers. If I said, "You're okay—you're not hurt!" they would nod even if blood was trickling down their legs. Mama knew when the water was too shallow to dive, when the drink was about to spill, how to build the perfect fort, and how to make an A on a book report. Life was simple then. I was a goddess on the home front, revered by my children for my mind-reading abilities, my talent for fixing broken toys, and my gift for reading aloud with different characters' voices. Those kids rushed the front door when they heard my key in the lock like I was Justin Bieber at a middle-school dance. My children were eager to share their thoughts and experiences with me, and they were anxious for my endorsement of every new endeavor. Those were good times.

Even back then, well-meaning relatives often dipped their oars into my parenting waters, but it wasn't hard to bring my kids into line. I'd say to them, "I know your grandparents let you do that, but who is the boss of you?"

"You are," they'd admit, reluctantly.

We called it "deprogramming" when my kids returned from an anything-goes grandparent outing. One of the hardest things to do as a parent is to stand up to one's own parents and tell them they can't do something with your kids because it is unsafe or unwise or simply because you have chosen to go another way. No matter how old the grandchildren, parents, and grandparents are when that happens, it's tough to do. Grandparents don't like to be chastised by their grown children—even when they're wrong and they know it. We'll probably be the same way when our teenagers grow up and have children of their own. At some point, you realize that, as an adult, you have to be your kids' parent, no matter whom you have to stand up to. It's part of the job description. Check the fine print.

Parenting offers some shining moments—birthdays, graduations, sports victories, award ceremonies, and lots of "firsts." But parenting is also cleaning up vomit when your kid has a virus, pacing the corridor while your kid has the broken bones in his arm realigned, and meeting your kid in the principal's office when you are more ashamed than he or she is. You don't get to pick and choose. It's all part of the ride.

The serpent in the garden is the friend in your kid's life who has no rules whatsoever. No curfew. No bedtime. No driving restrictions. He's free in the world and virtually on his own. Neglected kids come from all socioeconomic backgrounds. Some have nannies. Others have parents who are in crises of their own, incompetent, absent, neglectful, or downright mean. All of my kids have had at least one friend like that. Good kids can have God-awful parents, you know. It's just the luck of the draw.

At first, my kids thought those friends had it made in the

shade. My kids felt that, in contrast, they were forced to live in a harsh prison camp in the suburbs. After all, nobody makes those friends get up for church on Sunday morning. They are the envy of every teenager because they never have curfews or punishments. They can always sleep late. They don't have to go to school if they don't feel like it. They can go to R-rated movies whenever they want. They can stay up all night watching television. They're free to eat out all the time because no one ever cooks dinner at their houses. They're available to spend the night anytime. They're never hauled out of bed to do yard work, nor do they have to stay home to study. Over the years, I've heard every version of, "He comes to school whenever he wakes up," "She can wear anything she wants," "She can stay up as late as she wants," and "She just comes home whenever she feels like it. She is *so* lucky!"

The truth, of course, is that nobody cares enough about those kids to see if they've done their homework, to check that they're safely in their beds at night, or to make sure that their baseball pants are washed. You don't have to have a license or pass a test to become a parent. You don't have to plan for it. It's easier to get pregnant and have a baby than it is to adopt a puppy at the pound. You don't have to make your children a priority in your life. Heck, you're not legally required to do a good job at parenting, or even to try to do a good job. Scary, isn't it?

My kids were convinced that friends with no rules, no limits, and no parental supervision had the best gig going until something happened that made them realize that all that freedom was not necessarily a good thing. The realization came at different times with my kids, of course, but each one had an almost identical wake-up call, a day when they "got it."

My kids attend big public schools in our neighborhood. They're terrific schools, deeply rooted in the community. They offer award-winning academics, sports, and extracurricular activities. They are supported by thousands of volunteer hours from parents and big stacks of tax dollars. Each class looks like a television spot for diversity in color, race, religion, and ethnicity. My kids have learned valuable life lessons in their public-school melting pot.

At some point or another, each of my kids has had a classmate who said these words: "I wish I lived at your house." The first time I heard that, I thought it was a joke. I quickly realized that it wasn't. The emotion of that realization haunts me to this day. It changed forever how I parent.

In my oldest child's eye-opening experience with one of the lucky no-rules kids, he learned a life lesson. The classmate was seated at my kitchen counter after school one day. He was eating his way through my snack basket. It was his first visit to our house. He and my son were working on a project together for middle-school social studies. He was obviously shocked when my son went to the project drawer where we keep supplies like poster board, glue, scissors, glitter, markers, string, stickers, and anything else we find on the side of the road, in the junk mail, or in the trunk of the car that we think may come in handy one day for crafts. I like to think my husband and I are very "greenwise" with our repurposing of trash. My kids call us dumpster divers. In case you are wondering, that is not meant to be a compliment.

While I heated up the glue gun and sorted out some old magazines and catalogs for the kids to cut up, the new friend's eyes followed me all around the room. I couldn't figure out why he was staring. I'd actually made it to contact lenses and lipstick that day, so I didn't think I looked too scary. I smiled reassuringly and decided to feed him. That's generally a good way to bond with boys. First, I laid out grapes. The boys polished those off in no time. Then I made peanut butter crackers. Those vanished in the blink of an eye. My son was focused on braiding yarn hair on his puppet, so he wasn't too interested in snacks, but his guest was clearly starving. I opened a tin of cookies and shoved it toward him. He ate every crumb, pausing only long enough to wash the feast down with a quart of milk.

My son stopped his gluing/glittering frenzy to comment, "You sure were hungry!"

"Yeah. Do you have food like this every day after school?" the friend asked.

"Sure," my son said.

"You're lucky," his friend said.

When our guest left at twilight to walk home—alone—I made sure to invite him to come again.

When he was halfway down my front steps, weighed down by a backpack bigger than he was, he turned to me and said, "I wish I lived here."

On the way back to the kitchen, my son looked thoughtful. "Mom?" he asked.

"Yes?"

"I think he meant it, Mom. I think he really wishes he lived here."

"I think he meant it, too, son," I said. "You never really know how hard things are at someone else's house. Remember that. Everybody doesn't have what we have."

"Yeah," he said.

The second time it happened, my middle child got in trouble

at school for sharing his lunch with another student.

"Are you kidding me?" I asked his teacher. "How is sharing food a bad thing?"

"It's against the rules," she replied.

Sigh. Okay. I told him not to share food in the lunchroom anymore.

Later the same week, he was caught giving the lunch he'd brought from home to a kid in the hall. He'd ordered a lunch for himself from the cafeteria. I got another phone call.

I knew there had to be more to the story. I decided to fish for it. "Son, why did you ask me to make you a lunch if you were going to eat in the cafeteria?" I asked.

"I needed it," he answered.

"For what?" I asked.

"I had to give it to somebody."

"Why?"

"That way, he can take it home for supper," he explained.

"Why does he need to take your lunch home for supper?"

"Because there isn't any supper at his house."

That was it, the sum total of our discussion. My son shrugged his shoulders at me and walked away. He'd identified a problem and thought of a way to solve it. He didn't understand why the adults in his life were giving him a hard time about it. As you might expect, I got on the horn, and that teacher and I had a powwow.

By the time my children were teenagers, the kids in their lives with no supervision were easy to spot. Everyone knew who they were. My kids still complain about the rules at our house—which are way more strict and unreasonable than the rules at any other teenager's house in the whole entire world, as they will tell you with very little prodding. But they know they are loved.

It has become an inside joke.

"If I didn't love you so much, I'd take the easy way out!" I've been known to shout. "I'd be upstairs asleep in my bed! I sure wouldn't be staying up until one o'clock in the morning to smell your breath after the homecoming dance!"

"Could you love me a little less on Friday night, Mom?" my son has been known to ask, flashing a smile (which cost me five thousand dollars) that makes my knees weak. "I'm going to need a little slack on my curfew."

YOU CAN'T BELIEVE EVERYTHING YOU HEAR . . .

FROM OTHER PARENTS

1. "My daughter tells me everything. We're very close."

2. "My son doesn't really need to study."

3. "He didn't do anything wrong. It's those other boys who are trouble!"

4. "The coaches don't like my son. He's a gifted athlete."

5. "My daughter would never do anything like that! She's a good girl."

6. "Of course, I know where my son was last night! He was in his bed—asleep."

7. "My daughter would never say that! She is a sweetheart."

8. "All I want is for my son/daughter to be happy."

9. "Party? What party?"

FROM TEENAGERS THEMSELVES

1. "None of my friends has to make up the bed before school."

2. "Everyone else is going to the beach for spring break."

3. "Nobody cares about chaperons anymore except you."

4. "All of my friends have a car but me."

5. "Everybody goes to see R-rated movies."

6. "Nobody else's parents are going to be there."

7. "I don't need any help. I can handle the problem myself."

8. "I don't need to read the booklet. I already know how to drive."

9. "It's not really a date. We're just friends."

THE COMFORTS OF HOME

Laundry Laments

I can't seem to write a book without including a chapter about laundry. I am not sure what that says about me, but I don't think it is anything good. How interesting can my life possibly be if I spend this much time whining about laundry?

I live with three teenagers, so I have a staggering amount of laundry every single day. Someone has to do it. Sure, my husband throws in a load in his annual nod toward laundry-room equality. Theoretically, my children are old enough to do their own. If I were willing to stand over them with a whip and a chair, I could probably make them wash their own clothes, but it wouldn't be worth it to me.

Moms like me can fight only so many battles at one time. The model for our armed forces says that the United States of America should be able to handle two wars and a small skirmish simultaneously. Going to war bears a striking resemblance to child rearing.

Just as America had to keep worrying about the Germans when the Japanese attacked Pearl Harbor, parenting teenagers never offers the luxury of fighting one battle at a time. There are always long, entrenched, ongoing wars in addition to small dustups when you least expect them. It pays to keep your guard up and the alert status at DEFCON 1.

The more I think about it, the better the war metaphor works for parenting. For now, I'm concentrating on winning the war in the long run. I'm thinking big picture. I want my kids to be kind, responsible adults who take care of themselves and their families. I also want them to help those less fortunate than themselves. It's a lot harder than you might think to grow people from the lima beans they look like on the first ultrasound pictures in the obstetrician's office into six-foot-tall, tax-paying adults.

Navigating the teenage years is hard on everyone involved. Some days, I'm just happy if no one goes to the emergency room or the principal's office. Right now, I'm focusing on the biggies: upstanding morals, loyal friendships, good grades, smart money choices, active spiritual lives, and healthy minds and bodies. That means I have to let some things slide. I am going to teach them to do their own laundry eventually. Really. I am. It's on my to-do list for the summer before each of them leaves for college. That way, I won't actually have to watch them do it for long.

In the meantime, I live in four-loads-a-day laundry hell. My kids change clothes more often than Barbie and Ken. No kidding. Teenagers have a shocking number of clothes-specific activities. I often feel like I'm a costume designer to the stars. Football, basketball, baseball, gymnastics, cheerleading, dance—the costume changes go on all day long. Just keeping up with accessories like cheerleading ribbons, musical instruments, and sports equipment makes me tired. When my daughter was small, there is no telling how many hours I spent looking for two matching shoes for a ridiculously expensive American Girl doll. That is time I will never get back. No matter how many sports bags you give kids, they forget something important at least once a week—something you'll have to quickly take up to the school to avoid a fine, a demerit, a scolding, or a beating.

The demands of fast-turnaround laundry are especially tricky. When you're bleary-eyed at midnight trying to wash three loads of baseball clothes, you have to watch out for collateral damage. I ask again, for the umpteenth time: why in the world are baseball pants white? They are designed to slide in the dirt when used as intended. Ridiculous. I have been known to attack baseball and football pants with my own highly successful cocktail of stain remover, bleach, detergent, club soda, bathroom cleaner, profanity, and prayer. My arsenal of chemicals looks like I'm preparing to beat back an outbreak of Ebola in the jungle. It is entirely possible that I may be personally responsible for another gaping hole in the ozone layer because of all the environmental toxins I sprinkle, spray, and pour with reckless abandon.

At least once a week, one of my teenagers leaves something expensive—a cell phone, an iPod, or some other fancy gadget—in a pocket of an item headed for the washing machine, and the result is an expensive trip through the spin cycle. By the time I hear it clanging around in the dryer, it is too late for rescue. Since my kids have much nicer cell phones than I do, I am every bit as sad as they are when those state-of-the-art gadgets drown in the washing machine. When valuable cell phones, permission slips from school, and lip balms get waterlogged, guess whose fault it is? The teenager who failed to empty his or her pockets before tossing the item into the dirty clothes bin, you say? Of course not! Somehow, my teenagers always blame me for everything from rainy spring break holidays to acne breakouts during prom week. Of course, they know better than to blame me out loud where I can hear them, but I can tell they secretly believe it's my fault that they have homework on the same night the collegiate national championship football game is played.

I should really take it as a compliment that so many things are my fault in their eyes. Although my powers are admittedly great, I do not, in fact, control the weather, nor do I determine who makes the cheerleading squad. I assure you that I don't accept any guilt in such matters. I have a lot more sense than that. Also, as a little perk of the job, I keep all the cash I find in the pockets of dirty clothes—and I think you should, too. I like to think of it as a thoughtful tip for the laundress from the self-absorbed adolescents who live in my home.

When my kids were younger, I was especially careful about emptying their pockets. Little boys put anything and everything they encounter during their days into their pockets. At the very least, the contents are disgusting. Sometimes, they're downright dangerous. I've removed live, wriggling animals from my sons' pockets, as well as rusty nails, snotty tissues, wads of chewed gum, and something my son found in the park and assumed was a balloon. I've spent thankless hours picking out sunflower seeds from the teeny-tiny holes in my washing machine when I failed to empty baseball pants pockets before washing. I've washed a wallet with a brand-new driver's license in it, and a steady supply of single dollar bills, which suggests my teens are secretly moonlighting as valet parking attendants.

Now, I check movie stubs to make sure my kids aren't sneaking into porn flicks. I look at fast-food receipts to see what they're eating and where. I check to see if the time stamps on receipts match up with my kids' curfews. I read any notes I find. In my experience, it pays to be a nosy mom. You'd be surprised how often teenagers rat themselves out. My kids have no future in espionage. I am way sneakier. This pays off when I occasionally spot-check to see if they are actually at the parties they said they were going to attend. Teenagers could call you on their cell phones from Pakistan and say they're one block from home. How would you know? I think parents should insert GPS trackers under babies' skin when they're born, just like people do with puppies. I am not at all concerned about my teenagers' right to privacy. That privacy guarantee is inferred anyway. You can't point to a single line in the Constitution about it. I am sure the Founding Fathers would understand. Most of them lived with teenagers, too.

Laundry is a big job—like cleaning up an oil spill in the Gulf. Serving as the laundress for teenagers it is a lot like working as a mail carrier during the holidays. No matter how many cards and catalogs you deliver every day, more keep coming. It never ends. No matter how many loads of laundry I do, more is always waiting. It's overwhelming and discouraging.

The absolute worst part about laundry duty is that teenagers do not appreciate the fact that clean clothes reappear in their rooms each day as if by magic. They are quite comfortable with having a laundry fairy come in to quietly remove the clothes from the conveniently located hampers and return them the next day freshly laundered, pressed, and ready to wear. Well, who wouldn't like a laundry fairy? In a pinch, the laundry fairy offers overnight turnaround service for please-Mama-I-just-have-to-wear-it date outfits, and she often works a midnight to 3 A.M. shift during tournament seasons. Those are not union hours.

Do you know what the laundry fairy looks like? I'll tell you. Most likely, she's a menopausal, saggy-fanny, slightly overweight mom with yesterday's eye makeup clearly visible underneath her reading glasses from the Dollar Store. She is utterly unflappable. Bring her your stained and tattered garments, and she'll return them to you miraculously healed. You can't get that kind of service at a five-star hotel. Of course, there's a catch. The laundry fairy must have given birth to you and love you more than anyone else in the world to work under such appalling conditions.

Every day, I wade through an overwhelming pile of laundry thrown to the bottom of the basement stairs by my middle child in his one backbreaking (just ask him—I once caught him researching child labor laws on the Internet—like I care about that) morning chore. First, I separate the clothes by color. I even have a "special needs" pile that requires serious, up-close-and-personal attention. This is the moment when experienced mamas like me really shine. You wouldn't expect a sweet young mama to successfully remove a stain caused by blue Slushy, ground-in grass, and bicycle-chain grease. You need a battle-hardened, mean mama like me, a woman who is not afraid to spray harsh chemicals that come with warning labels that suggest blood tests every three months to check for liver damage.

Out of the kindness of my heart, I wash the clothes, fold them, place them in individual baskets *that have my children's names on them* (there was a week or so when I thought that was going to work), and deliver them upstairs to my kids' rooms at the end of each and every day. For this work, I think I should be nominated for sainthood. I'd be a shoo-in. The pope would put me on the fast track, for sure. I'd blow by the beatification requirement. I have amassed an impressive body of work. I think my kids should thank me on bended knee for all those clean clothes. It would also be nice if they wrote me thank-you notes, which would be especially meaningful if they included cash. I think it would be a smart move by my children if they kissed me on my cheek at least once a month and told me how much they love me and appreciate their clean clothes. I'd like that even better than cash. Don't worry. I'm not going to hold my breath waiting for that little fantasy to come true.

The little rodents do *not* appreciate their clean clothes or *anything else* I do for them on a regular basis. That's the nature of the beast. We didn't fully appreciate what our mothers did for us either, not until we were parents ourselves. Now, I think there should be a statue in my mother's honor at the very least, or maybe an airport named for her. It's not possible to appreciate your parents when you're still a teenager, and that is a crying shame. I hope that in retrospect, when they're grown and doing their own laundry and hopefully are not in prison, my kids will remember some of the sacrifices I made for them and be grateful. I hope they call me on the phone and tell me about that in elaborate detail while I sip on a cocktail and chuckle to myself. That could happen, right? Wouldn't it be fabulous?

Today, however, I'm a little worked up about the laundry. I feel like raising a big stink. And by the way, if I didn't do all the laundry every single day that rolls around—including national holidays and times when I'm sick, tired, or have way more fun things to do or work deadlines piled up on my calendar—there would be a literal stink in this house that you simply cannot imagine unless you have personally gotten a whiff of football uniforms left to marinate in the car for a few days in the middle of August in Alabama. I think a highly effective interrogation technique would be to shove those sweaty uniforms under the noses of suspected terrorists. I guarantee they'd cough up the WMD locations. Nothing is more pungent. In comparison, being sprayed by a skunk is a sashay by the perfume counter at the mall. Diaper pail fumes are a walk in a rose garden in June compared to the smell of sweat-soaked football girdles. I have gagged many, many times when loading my washing machine. It's a humbling experience.

Teenagers really do stink, you know. It's not just metaphorically true. There is nothing as low as the moment you have to tell your newly hairy teenager to take a shower because the B.O. is knocking you down. Of course, as soon as they figure that out—and as soon as they are interested in members of the opposite sex—they suddenly become the cleanest people on the planet. Two or three showers a day are common. They take their time in the shower, too. They make sure to use up every last drop of hot water and every ounce of your expensive spa products (the ones they gave you for Mother's Day). In fact, the more the shampoo or body wash costs, the more they use or leave upside down in the tub to slowly drain away. Money is no object to teenagers—as long as it is your money, of course. Their money is another matter entirely, one I address in another chapter right here in this book. Teenagers don't care about other people's showers. They don't even care if a sibling needs to get in that bathroom to throw up. They certainly do not care about your water bill. One of my kids was quite shocked to learn that residents are actually billed for water usage. I think he believed free water was guaranteed in the Bill of Rights somewhere.

This is the point where soak meets the spin cycle in this teenage laundry story. Do you think that my teenagers take those perfectly folded, beautifully ironed, pristine clothes and immediately, joyfully, and with genuinely grateful hearts put them away in their drawers and closets? Of course not! It seems like such a reasonable expectation to me—logical, too. I can tell you right now that if someone were saintly enough to wash my clothes, fold them, iron them, hang them, and return them to my own personal bedroom, I would have no difficulty whatsoever in completing the arduous task of putting them away properly. How hard can it be? It takes just a few minutes a day, tops. It's a job they could do while texting on their cell phones. We all know how crucial that is to their continuing to live and breathe.

Big theatrical sigh here. With teenagers, the obvious almost never happens. My teens go to great lengths to avoid simple compliance even when it would be good for them, too. They get to wear the unwrinkled clothes, after all. It becomes a test of wills that eventually results in an ultimatum from me: *You cannot leave this house until you put those clothes away!* All of that drama is so unnecessary! It's silly—like killing a roach with a bunker-buster bomb. I have been known to ask, "Really? This is necessary? I have to threaten you to get you to hang your clothes up?"

Here's what teenagers do best: They back you into a corner until you hear ridiculous things come out of your mouth that sound like your own mother. They make you so weary of the whole subject that you want to roll your eyes, too. They wear you down. It's a pretty good strategy, one used historically by outnumbered and under-equipped guerrilla fighters in small insurrections around the globe. Eventually, wandering bands of tribal clans wore out the Russian army in Afghanistan. It works. Sometimes, the big dogs simply give in to get past the issue already, whatever the cost.

Teens prefer to rifle through the clean laundry basket over the course of a week or so, fishing out favorite clothing items on an as-needed basis. After all the selecting and discarding, the previously folded clothing items resemble a basket of rags used to wash the car. I call this behavior the I'd-rather-live-out-of-a-laundry-basket-than-do-what-Mom-said choice. It's classic teenager. These are people who will happily cause themselves great inconvenience if by doing so they can make you suffer, too. It's a control thing.

The worst behavior in my household is so egregious it makes me feel slightly nauseated just writing about it. I am not making this up. I couldn't. I'm not that imaginative. On a regular basis, my children go to the trouble of transferring neatly folded piles of laundry on their beds to any other surface—the floor, a chair, or a desk—so they can sleep comfortably undisturbed in their snug little beds at night. In the morning, they move the clothes back to the freshly made beds. Of course, it takes twice as much time and energy to engage in this maddening campaign than it would to simply go ahead and put the clothes away properly. I can't explain why teenagers do things like this. It's like observing the mating habits of some strange species of frog in the rain forest. I fail to comprehend how I can be genetically related to human beings who behave so badly.

I guess the worth-it factor to my teenagers in this cost-benefit ratio is just how enraged their behavior makes me. My head has been known to spin around like a top. Fire shoots out of my eyes like I am a character in a comic book. My voice screeches through two octaves in outrage. I think my children enjoy the fireworks like a television reality show. It breaks up the day. Their behavior causes me to lose my already tenuous hold on hormonal surges of temper. I've seen my teens blow bubbles in my face with their gum and make sarcastic remarks to one another *while I am still ranting.* That's right. My kids make fun of me as I am standing there raising

Cain. It's all about what tickles the funny bone, I guess. I am here to tell you: Big Mama is not amused.

When my kids are caught in an early-morning time crunch, they solve the must-put-up-the-laundry-now-that-I-didn't-put-up-yes-terday-before-the-old-bag-starts-yelling dilemma more creatively. Even for the ungrateful wretches (as I lovingly refer to the teenagers I gave birth to myself), this is lower than a snake's belly. The first time it happened (yes, they've done it more than once, the little mon-sters), I refused to believe the evidence before my own eyes.

The morning began like any other. I began emptying the laun-dry hampers (because—surprise, surprise—my middle child for-got to perform his little chore again) right after getting my kids off to school. Guess what I found? You are not going to believe it. I found a pile of *clean* clothes crammed willy-nilly into the *dirty* clothes hamper! No need to reread that sentence. You read it cor-rectly the first time. Yes, ma'am, one of those children I carried around in my very own uterus really did that. To avoid the oh-so-terrible job of putting clean clothes away, my teen elected to skip the whole *wearing*-of-the-clothes stage and jump right back into the relentless, endlessly looping dirty laundry cycle.

You can probably guess what happened then. I completely lost it. For about a minute, I fantasized about showing up at the high school carrying the dirty clothes hamper from my boys' bathroom. In this fantasy, I planned to empty the hamper theatrically on one of my children's heads, preferably while he was surrounded by all his friends to heighten the public humiliation. I also con-templated the satisfaction I might receive from simply dumping all the clothes in my child's drawers out his bedroom window. Then I remembered how much those clothes cost me, and that fantasy ceased to appeal. I admit it: the discovery of clean clothes stuffed into the dirty clothes hamper lit me up like a Roman candle. I don't think I would have been any angrier if I'd opened a door and found my husband in bed with another woman. Truly.

I vowed on the spot that this foul injustice would not go unanswered. Determined to identify the culprit, I set out on my search with the zeal of a Nazi hunter. A bloodhound couldn't have kept up with me. I was out for Shakespearean-style vengeance. When I finally identified the little criminal, I planned to assign enough yard work to last until the kid qualified for Social Security benefits.

Another thing my teenagers do with clean laundry that makes me want to whack them over the heads with a tennis racket is that when they finally deign to push, squeeze, and poke the clothes into already overflowing, messy drawers, they make no attempt to refold, stack, or tuck so as to utilize the limited storage space in any useful or meaningful way. My children have actually gouged the furniture, caught the clothing on the backs of drawers, and forced the drawers on antique chests to close or open with brute force—to the distinct detriment of the furniture that I saved long and hard to buy.

They will apparently do anything to avoid a minor frustration that could have been solved with five minutes of patience and attention to detail. I've lost count of the number of drawers my kids have trashed like Huns sacking their way to the coast. They don't know the meaning of gentle persuasion or patient tugging. They go at those drawers like miners hacking their way into a vein of gold. *Jerk. Pull. Stuff. Slam.* I once came upon my middle child stuffing his blue jeans into a drawer at great expense to the hand-carved woodwork along the bottom of the chest. "Son, that chest survived the French Revolution and then made it another 150 years until you came along. Show a little respect," I told him.

Everything with teenagers is about instant gratification. When I finally throw a full-scale tantrum and forbid everyone from leaving their rooms until the drawers are reorganized, they do the most superficial job possible—the very least they can get away with upon inspection. Even if the clothes make it into a drawer, they are sure to be wadded up like newspapers used to ignite a fire. That's the way it is with teenagers. Every time I encounter another shocker and think to myself, *I don't actually have to say that, do I?* or *Anyone with good sense knows not to . . .* , I find that I do, indeed, have to say it. Over and over again. It is never enough to simply explain in a reasonable and logical manner what must be done, to give a clear rationale, and to expect it to be handled. This is how the cliché "Do it because I said so" came to be. "There can be only one general in the house," I tell them. "Think of me as a five-star."

These are the same people who text me from their bedrooms to ask when dinner will be ready. I have to threaten them with the loss of electronic devices before I can ensure compliance with the simplest of things—like hanging up wet towels. Think about it. How much can you really explain about the necessity of hanging up wet towels? It's what humans do. It's the kind of behavior that separates us from animals. It's self-explanatory to anyone with an IQ above freezing.

So, I ask myself, *how is it possible that I am involved in yet another conversation about wet towels and putting away the laundry?* The answer is clear. It's because teenagers don't care one bit about wet towels or clean laundry. They have different priorities. In order for laundry to move up in the pecking order of importance to teenagers, I've found that it is necessary to encourage them to embrace my priorities as their own. I find it's much easier to do that when I am holding their car keys, their cell phones, and their allowance hostage. Frankly, you have to be willing to go there. I am willing. I have three words for teenagers: bring it on. This laundry fairy is worn slap out.

YOU CAN'T TEACH TEENAGERS...

1. To change the toilet paper roll.

2. To throw away empty cartons of milk or juice. They leave one swallow and put them back in the refrigerator.

3. To use a coaster.

4. To apply sunscreen *before* going out.

5. To study for a test before the night before.

6. To floss their teeth, put the cap back on the toothpaste, and squeeze the tube from the bottom.

7. To turn the volume down—on anything.

8. To wipe the crumbs off the kitchen counter after snacking.

9. To put things back where they belong.

10. To do things right the first time.

11. To consider the long-term risks and benefits.

12. To hug family members in public like they mean it.

13. To be nice to the siblings they'll miss when they go to college.

14. To get up for church on Sundays without complaint.

15. To care about things that don't affect them personally.

16. To fill the car with gasoline *before* the warning light comes on.

17. To care for the dogs, cats, fish, ponies, hamsters, lizards, snakes, birds, rabbits, and every other creature, great or small, that they swore they would be *entirely responsible* for when begging their parents to adopt the animals in the first place.

Don't Look Under the Bed

I'm an extremely orderly, organized person. I have always been like this. I wish I were a more spontaneous, fun person. I love to hang around people like that, but I'm just not naturally one of them. (I also wish I were five-foot-seven and had long, red, curly hair, but that's not going to happen either. That ship has sailed. I'm over it.) What I am is nauseatingly responsible. You can count on me. I have a calendar and Band-Aids in my purse. I'm almost never late. (If I am, dial 911 immediately. Something bad has undoubtedly happened.) In fact, I'm usually a tad early because I am slightly pessimistic by nature, so I always assume that everything that can go wrong will go wrong. I'm usually right, too. I believe that it's best to be prepared for . . . everything. I always have batteries, bottled water, liquor, chocolate, and another book to read. That's all I really need.

As you might expect, I keep a tidy house. (Notice I did not say *clean*. Clean is another matter entirely, I'm afraid—a state of nirvana that is impossible to attain if you live with teenagers.) Everything has a place in my house. I like it that way. Other, less orderly people who live here and complain about cleaning up are grateful for my neatness compulsion when they want something in a hurry—like an extra roll of toilet paper, batteries for the remote control, a piece of poster paper for a project due the next day, or a new toothbrush because theirs fell in the toilet. Nobody whines about Mama then, let me tell you.

Some people (who share my DNA) say I'm a neat freak. How is that a bad thing? I've had the same pair of scissors on my desk since I was fifteen years old. I'm not confessing a fetish for office supplies or anything kinky like that. I mention this so you will understand that, thanks to my orderly nature, I rarely lose anything. Unlike the teenagers who share my roof, I put things back where they belong. After using the duct tape, I am one of those people who pulls out a little extra on the roll and folds it over on itself so no one has to find the start when it's needed again. As far as I'm concerned, that's how civilized people behave. I do not like to return to sleep in a bed that has been left unmade all day long. It doesn't feel right to me. I sweep my front porch every morning so my door looks welcoming to friends and open for business. Also, despite the fact that our eighty-year-old house obviously needs some work and the yard is one short step above embarrassing, I'd be ashamed for people passing by to think nobody lives here. We love our house. We're just too broke and busy raising children to pay much attention to an endless list of repairs.

What do you think happens when you take a neat-freak mother and give her three ordinary, decidedly non-neat-freak teenagers?

Nothing good, let me tell you. My kids' rooms are almost more than I can stomach. Honestly, it makes me feel physically ill to walk in there. I feel lightheaded and a little nauseous. It's the same feeling I get when I pass a car accident on the highway. My kids' rooms are way, way beyond messy. I don't know how they stand it.

"How can you live like this?" I ask them all the time.

"We don't mind," they always say with indifferent shrugs. "You should see our friends' rooms. They're much worse."

"I don't think that's possible," I reply.

I'm not sure I can do justice to the depths of their filth with a description in these pages, and I am pretty handy with adjectives. What human voluntarily lives in squalor? How can anyone get a moment's peace, comfort, or sleep in the midst of devastation? I swear to you that if we were robbed, I could not go in their rooms and tell if the thief had been in there looking for money or valuables. I would have no idea if anything was missing. That's because their rooms always look that way. I'd have to check the living room or my bedroom to reassure myself.

"Oh, thank goodness, officer, my mistake! We weren't robbed! It's just the normal mess!"

My teenagers' rooms look like they've been tossed by narcotics agents. Clothes literally litter the floor. It makes me feel short of breath just to open their doors and look in. When I walk through their rooms in the morning straightening, folding, turning lights off, putting things away, gathering glasses and garbage, picking up money found on the floor, moving expensive headphones, iPods, and other gadgets out of the path of their big feet, it never fails to infuriate me. I never get past it. I see thousands of dollars in clothing, technology, furniture, musical instruments, and other miscellaneous items tossed around with no regard for their well-being. I'm convinced teenagers never really learn to value material possessions until they have to pay for them with money they earn themselves. Talk is cheap. Minimum wage speaks loudly. (When my older son worked his first real job as a summer lifeguard, he learned some good life lessons. When he cashed his first paycheck, I pointed out, "Son, you worked one hour to earn what you spend on one fast-food lunch.")

My kids sometimes behave like spoiled rock stars who trash hotel rooms. No matter how many times I tell them not to eat in their rooms like animals in their stalls, I find half-eaten sandwiches, crackers, chips, and candy on tables and under beds in a sumptuous buffet for roaches. This food orgy for insects virtually guarantees a round of throwing up by any pet that roots out forbidden goodies left to ripen and rot.

I'm not one of those mamas who is willing to close the door and pretend the mess doesn't exist. I can't do it. I've tried. Our house is too small for that. Their messy rooms are on the ground floor, a can't-miss visual treat for any guest who walks in. It embarrasses me to death. When a guest asks to use the bathroom, I run ahead to make sure hand towels and soap are available and clean and that the sinks are free of toothpaste worms. Most importantly, I check to see that the toilets are flushed. Yes, indeed. I really have to see if my teenage children have remembered to flush the pee and poop. What a treat that is for me. As I've said on numerous occasions, I am way overeducated for my current position and seriously underemployed.

My teens know they aren't supposed to leave the house until their beds are made, their clean clothes are put away, and their rooms are tidied. So they do all that—after a fashion. Let's just say that they have low, low standards. Technically, they comply with my demands. The sheets, blankets, and comforters are pulled up to the tops of the beds—loosely speaking. Of course, huge lumps remain in the beds where they've pulled the covers over dirty clothes, a book or two, a pair of socks, or, one time, the family cat (no kidding) that was sleeping under the covers. They clear off the surfaces of their furniture by shoving everything in drawers or simply stacking debris like firewood in one big pile rather than the usual series of small, overflowing heaps of rubbish. They never actually go through those piles to sort, throw things away, or put things away properly. Never.

"It's clean enough, Mom! You should see my friends' rooms! They're so much worse than mine! I've never even seen _____'s bed, and _____ doesn't even use hangers anymore. He just picks something to wear out of the pile in the bottom of the closet. It's pretty cool, actually."

Most of all, I warn you like a first-timer at a horror movie: do not look under the bed of a teenager! I'm not worried about the *Sports Illustrated* swimsuit issue you might find. I'm talking about the literal filth that hides there. It's a lot like a trip to the city dump. Old toys. Stray socks. Dust bunnies the size of prairie dogs. Hair clips. Petrified Easter and Valentine's candy. (It really is too old to eat. I tried that once in a chocolate emergency. Trust me on this.) Old test papers. Books. Ticket stubs. Golf and tennis balls. Loose change. (I usually find enough change to make me wonder who harvests the coins from fountains. Could I hire those people on a percentage basis to clean out under my kids' beds? I could invest that change. Why are my kids so contemptuous of change? They never seem to use it. I'm not too proud to spend change. I have been known to count out ten dollars in change in the movie ticket line. It doesn't make me very popular, but I get rid of a lot of nickels and dimes that way. Money is money. It all spends the same.) I have also found half-eaten apples, my favorite hairbrush that one of my teens borrowed and never returned, and some completely unidentifiable brown globs of . . . I have no idea what. Katrina mold? Mushrooms? A shrunken head? A giant hairball? A mummified body part? There's no way to tell without a full crime-scene team to investigate.

When I finally reach the end of my rope with the under-the-bed mess, I rake it all out using a broom, a baseball bat, or a golf club—whichever is handiest. I would never stick my bare arm under one of my kids' beds. Anything could be hiding under those bedskirts. Bodies could be stashed there. After I rake the debris into a pile in the middle of the room, I bring two trash bags—one for actual garbage and the other for Goodwill. Then I hand those bags to the teenager who sleeps in that room and beat a hasty retreat to the sound of loud protests about the unfairness of that teen's lot in life. It would take about ten minutes to clean out under the bed properly. Naturally, that teenager spends at least fifteen minutes complaining about the job before finally tackling it.

Here's the thing that baffles me most. When the parent/teen wrangling is over, the dust has settled, and the rooms are finally clean (to my standards) and once again capable of supporting human life as we know it, don't you think that the teenagers who sleep there would do just about anything to avoid another you-have-to-clean-your-room battle by keeping them tidy? That seems like a logical reaction to me. I usually internalize life lessons fairly quickly, but I am sad to report that my teenagers have never learned the clean-room rule. It's as if neat-and-tidy is an unnatural state for teenagers' habitats. In just a few short days, the rooms usually return to their feral state. You can almost hear the jungle noises. Grownups need a machete, a teenage guide, and a tetanus booster to walk through the rooms.

Maybe that's the point, now that I think about it. Nothing says "Do Not Enter" to a grownup better than a big, smelly mess.

THINGS I HAVE FOUND IN MY TEENAGERS' ROOMS

1. Year-old thank-you notes that were never mailed.

2. Fast-food drink cup with mold growing on the lip.

3. Long-lost pacifier in the air-conditioning vent.

4. School forms that were never turned in, even though I stayed up until midnight filling them out.

5. Candy stash of staggering proportions.

6. Wads of cash stuffed into shoeboxes, as if my teens were secretly saving to pay off a future kidnapper.

7. A drawerful of used-up ChapSticks and lip glosses with no useful value for humans.

8. Hairy, unrecognizable former food products that looked like they belonged in a research facility.

9. Enough plain old garbage to fill a Hefty lawn-and-garden bag.

10. Clothing items outgrown at least three years ago.

11. Chewed gum stuck to the bottom of the bed frame.

12. Bloodied Band-Aids that were removed and slapped on to the nearest surface, the side of the shower stall, for example, rather than being thrown away in a sanitary manner.

13. A Mother's Day card my son was forced to write at school but never actually gave me.

14. A pirate's head cup containing a month's supply of daily vitamins, which I assumed my son had swallowed before leaving the breakfast table.

15. The expensive silk tie my son borrowed from my husband to wear to a dance and subsequently used like kitchen twine to secure his overflowing backpack.

16. The credit card I allowed my teen to swipe to fill his car with gas, now serving as a handy-dandy, easy-to-steal bookmark.

What's for Dinner?

Feeding hungry teenagers is similar to feeding wild animals at the zoo. I feel like I'm always throwing food over the fence in an attempt to fill up the animals. "Here you go!" I say, sliding a hot pizza onto the table. "No need to fight over it! There's more where that came from!"

Teenagers are bottomless pits. I don't know where they put all the food they eat. They're in great shape, of course. Just looking at a cupcake adds inches to my waistline. I can't indulge my sweet tooth nearly as often as I used to (every day) without having to wear my fat jeans (sometimes, it's worth it). At a bakery recently, I stared longingly at a glass case filled with mouth-watering treats. When the counter server asked what she could get me, I said without even thinking about it, "I'd like the top shelf, please." I meant it. I could eat my way through a dozen petits fours without breaking a sweat or taking a water break. I can't do that anymore without paying a control-top panties price. I hate control-top garments. When I wear them, I feel like a puppy that needs to tinkle every five minutes. Teenagers don't have to face consequences like that. They burn calories as fast as they consume them. The world is an unfair place. I think I've mentioned this before.

It is not unusual to hear my kids rustling around in the pantry less than an hour after I've finished cleaning up the kitchen and wiping down the counters for the two hundred and twenty-seventh time of the day. I always know it's they because it sounds like bears foraging for honey after a long hibernation. They knock boxes over, shove canned goods out of the way, crinkle bags, and generally hunt-and-gather in search of the perfect sugar-laden, carbo-loading snack food. "They can't possibly be hungry again this soon!" I always say, no matter how many times they do it. Keeping teenagers' bellies full is like feeding premature babies in the neonatal intensive care unit. Those babies expect some food to be thrown down their throats every two hours or so, or somebody is going to hear about it.

It is not uncommon for me to still be in the process of cleaning up the kitchen when one of my kids wanders back in for a snack. "You've got to be kidding me!" I have been known to shout while waving my sponge. "Out, out, out! The kitchen is closed for a few hours! Check back later!"

Many, many nights, I have been just about to drift off to sleep only to hear one of the wild-boar-like beasts foraging through the refrigerator or pantry with the desperation of a diabetic trying to ward off a sugar low.

"It's midnight! What could you possibly need now?" I yell downstairs.

"I'm having a bowl of cereal, Mom! You don't have to do anything!" one of my teenagers yells back, clearly affronted.

"Why did you wait until now? It's too late to eat! Can't you wait until morning?" I ask.

"Well, excuse me for being hungry, Mom!" replies the outraged teen. "I can't sleep if I'm hungry!"

They can't help it, of course. They really can't. Teenagers are hungry all the time. They are in constant motion. Think about it. Almost every activity they participate in involves exercise of some type. They play all kinds of sports like football, basketball, and baseball. They swim and hike and run for the fun of it. Remember those days? They walk everywhere like wandering bands of nomads. Cheerleading practices look like one long aerobic workout to me. Also, teenagers grow at shocking rates. Khakis that fit at Christmas are too short by Valentine's Day. They actually need all those calories and all that sleep. They're building muscles and brains. I wonder: how many Little Debbies does it take to make a brain cell? On second thought, I do not want to know the answer. No good will come from research into that foodlike product.

I'm sad to report that I continue to grow at an astounding rate, too. Apparently, my width hasn't quite caught up with my height. I am so jealous of the fact that teenagers can eat anything they want to without getting fat that I can hardly stand it. I used to be able to do that, too. It sure was fun while it lasted.

When I went out to lunch with my teenagers recently, I ordered a salad with low-calorie dressing and an unsweetened iced tea because of the previously mentioned weight/height discrepancy. (This is not my fault, since I am eating the same things I always have. I do not know what the problem is.) I despise unsweetened iced tea as only a Southern woman who thinks of sugared iced tea as a birthright can hate it. Drinking unsweetened tea puts me in a bad mood. I feel strongly that drinking tea without real sugar is, frankly, beneath me. I consider it a serious deprivation for a woman who has written an entire chapter on sweet tea (see book #1, *SWAG: Southern Women Aging Gracefully*). You don't want to get between a Southern woman and her iced tea, a Brit and her cuppa, or anyone from the Pacific Rim and a bowl of rice. Take away people's edible touchstones and they lose their bearings and begin to wonder about the meaning of life. Some foods are more than the sum total of their nutritional value. Some foods are culturally iconic.

After I placed my order, one of my kids ordered a medium pizza *for his own personal consumption*. He mulled over the sides for a few seconds before finally deciding on French fries. With cheese.

I almost gagged. "You are the poster child for poor eating habits today, son," I said.

"Fine," he responded with a long-suffering sigh. "Could you add a salad to that, please?" he asked the waitress, glancing pointedly at me. "And a glass of milk"—his *pièce de résistance*. "You happy now?" he asked me.

"Not particularly," I said. "Why didn't you order the onion rings? You know they make the best onion rings in the city."

"I didn't order onion rings because I don't like them. You're the one who likes onion rings, Mom. You just want me to order them so you can eat some. I'm not here to do your dirty work for you. You're a big girl. Order what you want," he said.

I scowled at him over the top of my reading glasses. The boy had me pegged.

"You have a lot to learn before you get married, son," I told him.

"What has that got to do with anything?" he asked, perplexed.

"It's just an observation," I responded.

When our pediatrician (God bless Dr. Linda Stone, who has kept me from quitting my day job on several occasions) asked about my kids' diets at one of their checkups, I told her the truth. If you look at what they eat on a single day, the state of Alabama might be tempted to remove our kids from our happy home. But if you look at their diets over a week's time, they're perfectly fine. I manage to slide plenty of fruits and vegetables in there. I am ashamed sometimes when I see all the prepackaged snacks and processed foods I dole out in addition to regular meals, however. Buying organic meat and milk isn't going to make up for all that, I know. I should be getting some kickbacks from Little Debbie. I've kept that wench in business for years.

It seems like every time I get in the checkout line with soda, Doritos, and Oreos, I'm behind a health nut. It is usually a super-thin woman (wearing workout clothes) who has a six-pack of bottled vitamin water, a head of cabbage, a carton of plain yogurt, and a pint of fat-free milk in her environmentally friendly, reusable bag. (How could I possibly use those? I'd need fifty at least!) Waves of disapproval emanate from her perfectly toned body when she glances at my groceries. I usually shrug off the guilt and try to hide the Oreos under my bag of prewashed lettuce.

Every month, my grocery bill runs neck and neck with my mortgage payment. Grocery shopping is one of the chores I despise most. I always end up with more than I meant to purchase, and I always manage to come home without the one item I went to the store to buy in the first place.

Also, grocery shopping on the scale necessary to feed teenagers hurts my back. Serious heavy lifting is involved. Although some grocery stores have bag boys, those people don't follow me home and unload my car. They're not allowed to. I asked. In addition, grocery shopping is often just plain embarrassing. I look like the little old lady in the shoe, who had so many children she didn't know what to do. In all honesty, I find that nursery rhyme a little too close to the truth to be amusing.

These days, here's how I shop: I cram groceries into my buggy until I can't wedge in another can of tuna. When I reach that point, regardless of where I am on my list, I consider it a sign from God and my checking account that it is time to go home. As you can imagine, by the time I round the last aisle, I am huffing and puffing because my buggy is heavy and hard to steer. It is filled to the brim with canned goods, fresh produce, cleaning products, cat food, paper goods, and five or six gallons of milk. When my kids were little, I never went to the grocery store without buying diapers. The rule was: get whatever is on the list, then add diapers. Now, it's milk. Teenagers drink a lot of milk. All those gallons make for a heavy grocery cart.

I have learned to lean forward over my arms and the top basket (where my children used to ride when they were small) and use my weight to drive the cart forward with my legs. You've seen football players do this in practice when they push those sleds across the field. It's especially hard to turn corners. A full grocery cart doesn't corner well at all. They should come with rearview mirrors and horns (the ones on clown cars would work well) to help navigate the aisles. Also, grocery aisles need passing lanes. I don't know why no one has ever thought of that before. It's hard to steer around the thoughtless shoppers who park their carts in the middle of the aisle while they compare the prices on every olive grown in Tuscany.

Sometimes, I get my feelings hurt at the grocery store. Perfect strangers comment on the contents of my basket all the time. I do not understand this. I do not editorialize about other people's grocery carts. I do not question why they need eight cans of shaving cream or twenty-seven jars of maraschino cherries. I'm curious about that, sure, but I have nice manners, and I know it is impolite to ask. It is not any of my business.

"Jeez, lady! How many people are you cooking for?" is a common dig. It's rude. It's not like I do this for fun, you know.

No matter how anonymous I would prefer to remain (sweatpants, no makeup, dark sunglasses), the bag boy greets me loudly by name when I enter. "Where you been all week?" Travis shouts. (Of course, I know his name. I told you I'm a nice person.) "I haven't seen you in three whole days!" he says. "That's some kind of record for you, isn't it?" It's the same joke every time. Let's just say I'm a good customer and leave it at that.

When I approach the checkout lanes, they often call for reinforcements. I swear I heard a cashier yell, "Incoming!" one time. Over the loudspeaker, I hear, "I need an extra cart on Lane 4, and some bagging help. Mrs. Thompson's here!" *Sure, tell the whole store about my private buggy business*, I think as I hunch over my cart in shame.

The fun doesn't end at the checkout. Things don't get one bit easier when I take my buggy out to the parking lot. It's only one step beyond the days of toting a skin bag and dashing home to the cave before being brought down by a bear. Unless you've personally experienced this, you can't imagine how hard it is to control a grocery cart when it's fully loaded with enough Gatorade and chips to keep a herd of teenagers happy for a week. Grocery carts are not engineered well at all. There's no space-age technology involved. To update grocery carts, I think we need to get whoever designed the nifty suitcases that spin and whirl on wheels so you can drag them around the airport with one hand. That would really help me out. Nothing has changed in grocery cart technology for a few world wars. At least one wheel is always cross-eyed and determined to go in a different direction from the rest, which requires strenuous manhandling—not one of my talents.

One day, I made the mistake of parking downhill from the grocery store. I learned a big lesson. I certainly won't do that again. It was not one of my finer moments. I barely lived to tell the tale. At first, I was delighted that the terrain was working with me instead of against me for once. As everyone knows, it is far easier to cruise downhill than to push uphill. I enjoyed the ease of my progress and felt like I'd caught a little break at the grocery store, like finding a two-for-one deal on spaghetti sauce. Unfortunately, my delight didn't last long. My buggy began building up a head of steam at an alarming rate. It took on a life of its own, gathering speed with every foot like a roller coaster headed down the first hill of a loop-de-loop. I wondered if my buggy was possessed by a demon. Nothing short of a priest or a calf-roping cowboy could have brought that thing back under control. Clearly, it was beyond my skills.

At first, all I felt was a smidgen of doubt about the forward momentum of my cart, but that soon blossomed into downright worry. As it sailed forward, the buggy pulled me along. The momentum shifted. I was no longer driving the food train. It was driving me. I was riding that out-of-control buggy like a runaway horse.

The first thing I tried to do to correct the problem was to hold on with my hands and pull back in a just-about-to-squat-down-on-the-ground position. That should have provided enough drag to stop a barge, but it didn't even slow the buggy. That's when I felt the first pangs of actual fear. Almost immediately, I realized I had another problem. I could no longer see over the buggy because I was so busy mock-sitting and pulling back with my arms stiff. I put both feet flat on the ground and began dragging them on the asphalt like I used to do when I was a little girl and I wanted to stop swinging. All that did was scuff up my new Joan and David flats and make me mad as a hornet.

I felt the first wave of panic roll through my body about then. I decided on a people-over-property response to the crisis. Although I could not see a way to protect the cart or its expensive contents, I felt a duty to the safety of grocery-buying citizens around me, so I took drastic action. With both feet, I jumped up on the rack underneath the buggy while still holding on and attempting to steer. My whole weight was on the cart now. It felt like a ride at the fair—the Tilt-A-Whirl, I think. My kids used to love to ride the grocery cart when they thought I wasn't looking. They'd kick-start it like a skateboard and then glide forward. But I wasn't having nearly as much fun as they seemed to. Of course, I fear pain much more than they do.

I soon gave up any hope of a dignified way out of the runaway cart scenario. I began yelling at shoppers in my way. "Clear out! Move it, sister! Out of the way! Coming through! Excuse me! Rogue buggy!" I shouted warnings at everyone in my path. I narrowly missed taking out a toddler who was totally fixated on the candy his mom had just unwrapped for him.

I could see a disaster in the making as a little old lady and her walker appeared on my radar at twelve o'clock. It was time for a Hail Mary pass. I tossed the giant pack of toilet paper off the top of my cart out in front as far as I could. I figured if I could just keep the Charmin in between my buggy and the little old lady, she had a chance of making it out of the collision alive. I continued to shout warnings at the top of my lungs. She continued to rummage around in her purse, completely oblivious to her impending doom. I felt like I was riding a meteor headed to earth in one of those disaster movies. At the last minute, I closed my eyes and prayed. I knew it was hopeless. No way was I going to be able to stop the grocery cart until it met an immovable object.

Time slowed. Somewhere in my brain, I wondered if the buggy would lose momentum when it hit the little old lady or whether it would just bump right on over her like a speed hump. I figured my final resting place would be the side of someone's car. I wondered briefly how much that was going to cost to fix, and if my insurance would pay for it or not. I hoped the car belonged to someone who would be nice about it. I wondered if I had my insurance card in my purse. I also hoped the impact wouldn't break the bottle of wine in my cart. I felt sure I was going to need it if I lived through the initial impact. Although the whole out-of-control ride lasted less than a minute, I had time to think all of those things. I swear it. Finally, I lowered my head and braced it on my arms like flight attendants tell you to do right before impact in an airplane crash.

That's when my runaway grocery cart met an immovable object. It wasn't the little old lady. Hallelujah! It wasn't an expensive car. Even better! I opened my eyes and looked right into the face of one of my older son's friends from the football team. He'd spotted my out-of-control buggy from the parking lot and sprinted over to help. What a good boy!

"Hey, Mrs. T! You okay?" he shouted from the spread-eagle

position he was holding in front of my cart, which he dragged to a halt with sheer brute strength.

I lifted my head. "When I get home, I'm going to bake you something delicious," I told the boy.

"Excellent! I like your pound cake a lot," he hinted.

"You got it," I said.

He walked away laughing and texting someone on his cell phone. There was no question that story was going to be all over town by nightfall.

Feeding a houseful of teenagers and their friends is a lot of work. It's shockingly expensive. Sometimes, it's dangerous. Just loading up all the bottles of Gatorade and water to feed the football team a single meal is a recipe for back pain.

Once you give birth to children, you're obligated to feed them, you know, no matter how exhausting and expensive it is. I always say that the reason all of these children keep hanging around our house is because we continue feeding them. It's like feeding any wild animals. They'll keep coming back for more.

On the bright side, as long as teenagers show up to eat, I know where they are, and that is a recipe guaranteed to make me happy.

THINGS TEENS SAY THAT ENRAGE THE COOK

1. "I like it better when we eat out."

2. "I forgot to tell you I have to eat with the team tonight."

3. "Are we having anything good for lunch?"

4. "I'm not hungry. I just ate with my friends."

5. "We're always out of ice cream!"

6. "Can I just have dessert?"

7. "Maybe I'll try some later."

8. "What is this supposed to taste like?"

9. "Can I be excused? I made other plans."

10. "Can I have something else instead?"

11. "So-and-so's mom makes this better."

TEENS ON THE LOOSE

Where Are You Going Dressed Like That?

I t all started with the red-glitter shoes from Target. My daughter was three years old, and she was obsessed with Dorothy from *The Wizard of Oz*. Recognizing a good thing, Target raked in the bucks selling Dorothy shoes to little girls. They were charming. Those shoes would tempt the tootsies of any female with a pulse. If they came in sizes big enough for me, and I could think of a single place I could wear red-glitter shoes without getting myself talked about, I'd have bought a pair myself. I wish I'd owned stock in Target when it first began selling those shoes. They flew off the shelves. Every little girl in America wanted a pair. My daughter loved them more than anything else in her wardrobe. As her feet grew, I combed the stores for bigger and bigger sizes. In the attic, I still have the first pair she wore. Because she loved the gritty sound they made when she rubbed her feet together, the sides are bald and shiny.

In our family, my daughter's Dorothy shoes represent our clothing Fort Sumter—the first skirmish in a long clothing war that is still being waged today. It was a sign of things to come. If you've never argued with a three-year-old about whether or not she can wear Dorothy shoes to church, you have no idea how formidable an adversary a baby girl can be. Think about trying to pull a fast one on Margaret Thatcher. It can't be done. Little girls know how to dig in. They can outwait you. They are hard to embarrass, and they do not appreciate the nuances of compromise.

I was unprepared for fashion controversy. Since my older children are boys, a keen interest in clothing was new to our house. When they were little, my boys could not have cared less what they put on their bodies as long as it was comfortable and went on fast so that they could get outside to play as soon as possible. I am sorry to say that their indifference to fashion ended in high school when they both discovered their inner clotheshorse. From then on, those boys lusted after expensive sunglasses, brand-name shirts, cashmere sweaters, silk ties, and hand-sewn moccasins. In the South where I live, young men's clothing comes with dry-cleaning bills from hell or hours of starching and ironing. It's hot down here. Boys sweat. You do the math.

My daughter's first fashion statement was simple. She wanted to wear her Dorothy shoes every single day, no matter what. If we were headed to the pool, she coordinated her swimwear with the Dorothy shoes. She was convinced she looked fabulous. Nothing I said changed her mind in the slightest. Every day, the shoe selection was a given. The only question became, "Do I look more beautiful in this dress, Mommy, or that dress?"

Don't you love the self-confidence of a little girl who can ask that question with a totally straight face? I wish girls kept the confidence they have as toddlers all the way though middle school and high school. That would sure come in handy when mean girls tear them apart. How do girls go from thinking everything they try on makes them look beautiful to doubting that they look pretty in anything? It just about breaks my heart.

If my daughter wore her Cinderella nightgown, she didn't need glass slippers. In her opinion, the red-glitter shoes were bound to look good. Shorts, dresses, pajamas, tutus, an occasional tiara, red-glitter shoes, and . . . nothing else. Bare bum. Naked as the day she was born. This fashion statement was confined to our house. I was a real stickler about that.

I tried to be understanding. I like to wear what I think makes me look my best; why wouldn't my daughter? Most of the time, it didn't matter one bit if she wore her Dorothy shoes wherever we were going. We rarely go anywhere exciting. She had cute regular clothes. I made sure that I purchased only choices that I could live with, which gave her an illusion of control. She got to pick out what she wanted to wear each day. However, since I'd approved all the choices, she couldn't get too far off the reservation. She had a penchant for beads, glitter, and jewel-encrusted trim—an over-whelmingly bedazzling fashion statement that was more appropri-ate for a retiree in Miami than a little girl.

One problem I never anticipated: having to enforce the se-lection of seasonally appropriate attire. If it's cold outside, you'd think kids would know instinctively that they can't wear summer clothes, right? If it's a hundred degrees in the shade, you'd think my daughter wouldn't dream of sticking her feet in fur-lined UGG boots, correct? You'd be wrong. Kids don't care about mi-nor weather-related details. They don't care if it's raining so hard there's a flash-flood alert. If they have new suede boots, they will still want to wear them to school. Teenagers, girls especially, want to wear what they want to wear when they want to wear it. They expect their favorite outfits to be clean, pressed, and ready to go at all times. They expect five-star valet service, and they never tip. As you might expect, this causes some tension on the home front.

You can't get away with dropping off your kid at school when it's seventeen degrees outside and she has chosen to wear shorts, flip-flops, and a halter top. First of all, there is the little matter of frostbite. Second, it takes just one phone call to stir things up at DHR. Third, it's horribly embarrassing. I learned to remove the off-season clothing options from my daughter's closet to avoid the beachwear-in-January discussion altogether.

The best thing about little girls and fashion is that they generally look adorable no matter what they wear—with one big exception. Children should never be dressed up like miniature adults unless it's Halloween, when countless princesses and Miss Americas pop up on every street corner. When I see little girls draped in hoochie-mama tank tops, fanny-hugging leggings, and four-inch heels, I immediately judge the parents guilty of something felonious. Like mother, like daughter, I always say. Here's a memo to those of you who missed this news flash: little girls should not look as if they are dressed by Whores "R" Us. *Sexy* is not a word you want bandied about when describing your kid's sense of style. It's creepy, dangerous, and tasteless. And while I'm on this soapbox, let me go ahead and say that little girls don't need makeup either. Their cheeks are rosy. Their lips are perfectly formed cherub's bows, and they have no lines or wrinkles. Even if their cheeks are sallow, their lips are barely visible, and they are pale as ghosts, they still don't need makeup. This is the only time in their whole lives when it really doesn't matter what they look like. When I see a twelve-year-old girl made up to look thirty-five, I immediately suspect that an aging-beauty-queen mama is trying to relive some unfulfilled dreams of her own. That is just icky.

When I see a teenage girl dressed like a ho, I think to myself, *That's mighty tacky.* If someone I like to gossip with is sitting next to me, I say out loud, "That's mighty tacky." I assume the girl has clueless or absentee parents. If you allow your teenage daughter to leave your house dressed like a ho without throwing yourself across the threshold to prevent it, you're not doing your job. In between the professional escort look and a full burka is a lot of room for personal expression. There has to be one outfit that you and your teenager can agree on. I know it's hard. I feel your pain. But that doesn't give you any excuse to bow out of the conversation. Pick your battles carefully. Remember, you're out to win the war, not every battle. But when you have to, get in there and fight! Your daughter will thank you for it one day. (You may have to wait a while. Parenting is all about delayed gratification and long-term investment.)

When my daughter was an infant, I suspect she deliberately spit up sweet potatoes or green peas on any outfit she found distasteful so I would have to change her before taking her out in public. That's a fairly sophisticated ploy for a non-walking person. Nowadays, she rolls her eyes, stomps around, and slams her bedroom door to make her point. I am regularly unmoved by such displays. This is not my first fashion show.

We had our first real difference of fashion opinion one Easter Sunday morning when my daughter was still immersed in her love affair with Dorothy shoes. She thought the $7.99 red-glitter shoes looked perfect with the hand-sewn, French-smocked dress with exquisite lace that took three months for nuns in a Greek convent to make and cost me half the month's grocery budget to buy and two hours to iron. I heartily disagreed. Rock met hard place. Mountain met deep blue sea. She wasn't budging. Neither was I.

"I want to wear my Dorothy shoes!" my daughter demanded loudly and theatrically. She was Evita Perón standing on a balcony, appealing to the masses. Her feet were spread wide. Her hands were on her hips. She was not giving in without a fight. She was sugared-up with candy from her Easter basket and ready to rumble.

"You know you can't wear them to church, sweetie. They don't match your dress. You can wear them when you get home," I explained. I wanted her to know the decision was non-negotiable but wouldn't last forever. It isn't wise to give a three-year-old much wiggle room in a standoff situation.

"But I *want* to wear them to church. They do *too* match! They match everything!" she exclaimed, gesturing dramatically to her wardrobe door as if to emphasize the importance of red-glitter shoes to the fashion industry as a whole.

I was through discussing. However, I sure didn't want tensions between North and South Korea to erupt into an all-out shooting war on Easter morning. I had other fish to fry and less than an hour to get everyone to church on time.

"How about if we take them with us in your bag? You can't wear them, but you can keep them with you."

"Nobody will be able to see them in my bag!" she wailed, as if I was somehow confused as to the purpose of shoes in general. She was clearly unwilling to be appeased.

"True," I said, "but you'll know they're there, and you'll have them ready to wear after the service is over. You can put them on in the car."

My daughter paused to consider her options. I continued wiping down the kitchen counter and let her. At one point, I saw her lips begin to jut out in a pout, and I knew she was contemplating throwing a full-scale tantrum, something absolutely not allowed in our household. She balled up her fists, opened her mouth, and took a deep gulp of air like she was preparing to let loose with a blood-curdling scream. I paused with the sponge and made eye contact with her. Not a flicker of a smile crossed my face. I did not utter a single word. I watched her face as she made her choice. She whirled around and stomped back to her room to change shoes.

"Wise decision," I said to my daughter's three-year-old back.

I repeat: you can't argue with toddlers. You have to outsmart them. If you can't do that, you're not wily enough for the job. The same thing is true for teenagers. If you have kids and no backbone, I suggest you buck up fast. Kids can sense weakness from their bassinets. They can smell it on your breath like peanut M&Ms. They know instinctively how to weed you out from the herd and take you down.

Tantrums never worked at our house. I *never* rewarded a tantrum in any way, even if it was over something the kid was going to get anyway. I don't care if the kid was screaming for a vitamin. If a tantrum was involved, nothing would be forthcoming. Period. I'm convinced this is the reason my kids never went through the tantrum stage. They knew instinctively that it would be a waste of time. My parenting policy is to not give in to the demands of terrorists. I know that if I do, it will come back to bite me on my fat fanny at the most inconvenient moment.

One of my kids' friends tested this policy at our house one afternoon.

"Does she mean it?" the friend asked my son.

"She always means it," he replied. "My mom doesn't bluff."

He got that right.

We made it past the red-glitter-shoe stage. However, the clothing wars continue to this day. Each year brings new fashion challenges. Currently, the battle rages over Nike gym shorts my child would like to wear to every event she attends, whether they are appropriate attire or not. I understand that teaching children to dress for work, church, school, and social events is part of the parenting job description. Like so much of parenting, it isn't one bit of fun.

It didn't help that the last time I forced my child into appropriate piano-recital attire, a lazy parent sat right next to me with her kid dressed in hot-pink and lime-green Nike gym shorts. I wanted to smack her and her kid. My child skewered me with a glare that would have undoubtedly turned me to stone if she had known how to cast the spell. I ignored the look and sighed.

"You look beautiful," I told my daughter.

She rolled her eyes. "I didn't want to look beautiful," she said. "I wanted to wear my gym shorts."

"She only wants to wear shorts these days!" the I-just-want-my-kid-to-be-happy parent leaned over and whispered in my ear. She shrugged her shoulders with a what-can-I-do-about-it gesture toward heaven.

You can do plenty, I wanted to tell her, but I didn't. I just smiled politely. My job is to teach my kids to do the right thing, regardless of what other people do. I just wish other people wouldn't make my job so much harder than it has to be.

Boys are easy to dress. They wear little boys' sizes until they outgrow them, and then they wear men's sizes. Simple. Once they graduate to a blazer, khakis, and a dress shirt, that uniform stays the same for the rest of their lives. Add suits for work, a tuxedo, and gray slacks, and men are good to go. My father, husband, and boys wear clothes that are remarkably similar. Sure, there are youthful distinctions. My sons look rakish in bow ties, but my husband can't pull it off. He would look like a cinched-up garbage bag in a bow tie. Some fashions, even for men, look best on young, triangle-shaped bodies. In general, however, the male wardrobe comes fairly standard.

Girls are another matter entirely. Since it is impossible to find clothes that fit me anymore, I thought it would be easy to clothe my teenage girl. Everything I try on seems more suited to her body and taste. Everything I see for sale seems to be cut for a teenage body, not one that has been stretched out to carry nine-pound babies. Every dress I try on is too short for me to bend over without revealing my granny panties. I assure you that sight would thrill no one. Don't even ask me what in the world has happened to women's T-shirts. I have no idea. They are now teeny-tiny. The cut is called "form-fitting." Whose form? They look great on my size-zero daughter, but when I try them on, they cling lovingly to each of my fat rolls. This is not a good look for me or anyone else my age. Also, the T-shirts are so long! I'd need a torso like Uncle Sam to use up all that material. If I buy a unisex T-shirt, the neck strangles me and smashes my bosoms flat. This issue has just about worn me out. If you have any ideas, I'd like to hear them.

The biggest conflicts arise over clothing selection. Teenage girls are particularly sensitive to anything that makes them look like "babies." Why are young people always in such a hurry to grow up? Comfort is not a priority. It's a fashion-first mentality. Since most designers sew for anorexic-looking six-foot-tall models, the average teenager has to adapt that look for the real world. This leads to arguments about dress and skirt length. Most schools have a "fingertip" rule. No dress or skirt can be shorter than the student's fingertips when her arms are at her sides. You can't believe the unnatural ways girls will contort their bodies to convince their moms that the skirts they want to buy meet the school dress code requirements.

Other arguments sprout up over cleavage, bare shoulders, sheer v. opaque, and heel size. There is no end to the variations in girls' clothing, so naturally there is no end to the number of contentious fashion points to be negotiated for every social occasion. The selection of a prom dress has forced many a mother to bed with a bottle of Tylenol and an ice pack. Feathers have flown; shoes have been flung; doors have slammed; hairbrushes have banged. Fathers have been forced to toss both daughters and mothers over their shoulders to carry them off to their respective bedrooms for a cooling-off period.

I've already told my daughter that she is wearing my wedding dress when/if she marries. It was my mother's before me, and if it was good enough for both of us, it will be good enough for her. I don't care if she has to alter every stitch in it. If it's too short, we'll add a ruffle. If it's too long, we'll cut it off. Every girl's a sucker for the big meringue. It will be lovely, I promise. No way can we survive shopping for a wedding dress together. There isn't enough liquor in the whole wide world.

My boys are skilled at avoiding being drawn into fashion discussions between my daughter and me. They know better than to pick sides. They are determined to remain as neutral like Switzerland. When asked for their opinions, which may require them to look away from ESPN's *SportsCenter* for a few seconds, they mumble that they don't know which shoes look better. If pressed, they shrug and say, "They both look fine to me. Wear whichever ones you like better." This complete lack of interest usually results in a mother or sister flouncing off in a huff.

On a positive note, however, when a mom or sister gets an honest-to-God compliment from a son or brother in the household, it's the real deal. You can take it to the bank. When I came down the stairs recently dressed rather stylishly (for me) for a television interview, rather than in my customary sweatpants and Saints T-shirt, one of my sons stared at me with big, round eyes so long the Coke ran over the top of the glass he was filling, which is as fine a compliment as I have ever received.

"Wow, Mom, you look great . . . like a real person!"

"Thanks!" I said, resolving on the spot to bake that boy a pie.

I take my compliments where I can get them these days. They are few and far between. You can't be too picky if you're hoping for praise from a teenage boy and you're over the age of consent. In general, adult women are simply invisible to teenage boys.

When my daughter was a toddler, if she saw that my fingernails were polished, she immediately suspected I was leaving town for business or pleasure.

"You going to a hotel, Mommy?" she'd ask, holding my hand and examining my French manicure up close, one finger at a time. "I like hotels, too, Mommy! I want to swim in the pool," she'd remind me in a wheedling voice.

In the scheme of scary, this-could-happen-to-me family scenarios like unplanned pregnancies, drug problems, failing grades, or criminal behavior, clothing clashes really aren't that big of a deal. I realize that. This doesn't mean, however, that a parent/teenager what-to-wear power struggle doesn't feel like the end of all civilized communication at the time. This, too, will pass. My grandmother used to tell me that when I was a teenager. It irritated me then, and it irritates me now—which doesn't make it any less true.

Parenting teenagers is a life of triage. You have to accept that premise when your oldest child turns thirteen. Most importantly, you have to make sure your kids breathe in and out and their hearts continue to beat every single day. Sometimes, just the knowledge that they are alive and well is enough. In a world with so many dangers, asking for anything more sometimes seems greedy.

But when things are sailing along as smoothly as they ever do in a household with teens, I have opportunities to address lesser issues, too. I ask (some would say "interrogate") my teens, "How are your classes going? Are you going to be able to support your family one day with those grades? What's going on with your friends? Do you realize how much your brother/sister loves you?" Eventually, all the big stuff gets handled—one way or another, for good or for ill. Then it's time to address the minutia.

My teenagers need to know things—like whether or not I will actually have a heart attack if my daughter wears flip-flops to her grandmother's funeral. "Count on it," I tell her. It's hard to predict life with hormonal teenagers and a menopausal mother. It's a volatile mix. I might take those flip-flops off my child's feet and beat her over the head with them. Real life is full of risks. My teenagers have learned that life lesson well. They live in fear of Mom. I think that's a good thing.

CLOTHING COMPLAINTS

1. "If I have to wear that, I don't want to go!"

2. "Do you want me to look like a nun?"

3. "I'll be the only guy there in a coat and tie."

4. "If you pick it out, I probably won't like it."

5. "It's not too short."

6. "Everybody wears it like this."

7. "Nobody wears that anymore."

8. "I don't know how that hole got there."

9. "I left my jacket somewhere."

10. "Mom, what did you do with my _____?"

11. "I don't have anything to wear!"

12. "My swimsuit *is* pulled up."

13. "I like to wear it this way."

14. "You are so old-fashioned."

15. "Mom, what look are you going for with that outfit?"

Can I Drive?

Teenagers genuinely believe they are immortal. If you have doubts about that, ask them yourself. Grab a random teenager from the nearest sidewalk. It doesn't have to be one of your own. He or she will tell you the same thing Dustin Hoffman tells Tom Cruise in the movie *Rain Man*: "I'm an excellent driver." Of course, the next part of that quotation is also true. Hoffman's character, Raymond, adds, "Dad lets me drive slow on the driveway."

Unfortunately, teenagers don't drive slowly on the driveway. They've moved past plastic coupes and battery-powered Jeeps and Barbie cars. That starting flag has been lowered—permanently. Teenagers drive real cars purchased with real cash. They fill those cars up with tank after tank of gasoline, which is like pouring liquid gold down the drain. Teenagers use more gas driving around doing nothing than any other group of humans on earth.

Go ahead. Ask your teenagers where they're going this weekend. They'll say, "Nowhere." Ask what they're planning to do. They'll say, "Nothing." Ask who is going with them. They'll say, "No one." Illuminating, isn't it? Teenagers are the only people in the world who can use an entire tank of gasoline in one weekend without going more than five miles in any direction.

Teenagers are not excellent drivers, statistically speaking. They're inexperienced, obviously. They're also easily distracted, like dogs when a squirrel runs across the road in front of them. One pretty girl or cute boy walking down the side of the road can cause a pileup. Did you know that the more kids they cram in their cars, the more likely they are to be involved in an accident? It's true. It makes sense, when you think about it. The more friends, the more distractions the driver has. Think about how loud a group of six teenagers is in your basement when they are all laughing, yakking, and wrestling with one another. Now, think about loading that same group into a car and handing them the keys. How safe does that sound to you? It makes me feel like I'm going to vomit. Filling a car with teenagers is like shoving an open box full of puppies into a car without their mama. That's exactly what a carload of teenagers without adult supervision seems like to me. On the surface, it looks like a whole lot of fun. But really, it's just asking for trouble.

When more than one teenager occupies a vehicle, there are bound to be arguments over music selection and who gets to ride shotgun. Those arguments can get physical. Bodies may be tossed over the seat or shoved out the door. I shudder just thinking about those long, late-night road trips to the lake and beach. Also, teenagers always leave about ten minutes later than any mature person in his or her right mind. They are unconcerned about traffic jams.

They are completely confident that they won't encounter any detours, accidents, or delays. They leave the *exact* amount of time needed to drive to their destination, with no wiggle room or margin for error. Then they have the audacity to be outraged if they are delayed in any way.

"It's not my fault I'm late! I left in plenty of time! It takes eleven minutes to drive there from here. Why did they pick that street for roadwork? It's totally unfair!" they screech, as if the Department of Transportation goes out of its way to make life difficult for teenage drivers.

I never thought I would say this (yet another item in the long, humbling list of things I never thought I would say or do), but music may be the most dangerous driving distraction for teens. Don't panic. I haven't joined a new anti-music cult. It's not that I think kids who listen to loud music are headed to hell on the expressway. It's not their souls I'm worried about here. (Although if you haven't gone through the playlist on your kid's iPod, you need to do that ASAP. I had to ask my husband to explain some pornographic lyrics in a rap song one time. Once I grasped the anatomical references, it made me blush, and I've been married for nearly twenty-five years. Stay on top of the music they download on the computer. You will likely discover some potty-mouth songs that would embarrass a sailor. I can only assume that rap singers have very limited vocabularies. Otherwise, they would not have to resort to such vulgarities as space fillers in their songs. Profanity is the stuff of small minds, I always say.)

The problem is that teens can't hear anything else going on around them when they crank up the tunes. If teenage drivers cannot hear ambient noises, they can't respond to auditory warnings in a timely manner. If they can't hear the police siren, they don't know to pull over, and that can't possibly end well. If they don't hear the tornado siren, they don't know to abandon the car and dive in the closest ditch. If they can't hear other drivers and pedestrians—as well as see them—they'll miss out on important clues to help keep themselves and other people alive.

When a pedestrian crossed against the light one afternoon and came within a hairsbreadth of being mowed down by my teenager, my son was outraged—not at the close call with death but by the fact that the pedestrian had clearly flaunted the rules for safe passage across the street.

"It's not his turn to cross, Mom! He can't do that!" my son said in righteous indignation.

"You're right," I said. "He should definitely have waited for the light. However, that doesn't mean it's okay to run over him just because he jaywalked. It's not a death-penalty offense."

If the music is so loud that people can hear it outside the car, it's like voluntarily making oneself deaf, I tell my kids. I promise you that if a teenager pulls up to my house with the car windows rolled down and the stereo blasting, he or she is responsible for babysitting any neighborhood children who are awakened from their naps. My bet is that spending an afternoon with a toddler who missed his or her nap will turn a music-blaring teenager into a monk with a vow of silence in a matter of hours.

This car-stereo discussion brings up another important question: why do teenagers always turn the music in their rooms or cars up so loud? It's one of the great mysteries of teenage life. Their ears are still sharp, so it can't be that. Is it the assumption that everyone else wants to listen to what the teenagers want to hear? That is quite erroneous, I assure them. How often do you enjoy the same music your kids listen to? Sure, it happens sometimes, but not often. First of all, if we grownups like the music they've chosen, that is almost enough of a reason right there for the teenagers to find fault with it. If I like the Avett Brothers and Amos Lee and needtobreathe (I do) just like my kids, I think that probably makes them question their own taste in music. Bottom line: since when do teenagers care what we think about anything?

I believe the reason for the loud music is probably the same one behind almost everything else teenagers do. There isn't a good reason. It's a whim. It feels good at the time. It's fun. These people have poor impulse control.

Teenagers' brains aren't fully baked. Studies by serious academics have tried to determine the exact age when human brains fully mature and become capable of wise decision making. (I could have informed those scientists that teenagers aren't ready for prime time, no matter what they tell you. I don't know why we spend vast sums of money to prove theories we already know are true. What a waste of green!) Guess what those studies have uniformly concluded? Teenagers are physically incapable of making decisions in the deliberative manner we ask them to. It's a lot like yelling at a one-year-old for wetting the bed. Your kid may have the IQ of Albert Einstein. It doesn't matter. You can't potty-train a one-year-old. They're not ready. (Yes, I've read about some of those competitive parents who potty-train their kids like precocious circus monkeys. There are freaks in every species. I do not have time for those people. I am writing about regular people in this book.)

One of the reasons we need young men and women in the military (besides the facts that their reflexes are amazing, they can eat anything that doesn't bite back, and they recover quickly from injuries, of course) is that their brains allow them to do dangerous things without reining them in. We call this behavior "bravery" in wartime. In peacetime, we call it "being a teenage idiot." "Hey, wait a minute, now," is a cautionary trait we develop with maturity.

One look at insurance rates will clue you in to the statistics. The first time you see how much your insurance premiums will increase when your teenager gets his shiny new driver's license, the sticker shock will make you sit down and put your head between your knees to avoid keeling over in a dead faint. It would be cheaper to buy tickets to Disney World and ride the monorail to the Magic Kingdom every day for the rest of your life. More fun, too.

Like many parents who want their kids to learn driver's education from a professional, I signed my oldest child up for a class at school. What a crock! Imagine how pleased I was to learn at the end of the first day's instruction that the teacher had ridden to class on a motorcycle (we call them "donorcycles" in our house) without a helmet. He also bragged that he could "get it up to ninety-five on the open road." My son was gleeful. I was peeved in paisley.

In my ongoing campaign to scare my children into being safe drivers, I reported my insurance agent's claim to my son that there is a 100 percent chance he will be involved in some sort of accident as a teenage driver.

Naturally, he responded by explaining how that statistic is mathematically meaningless. (Those stupid AP math courses make me look dimwitted. I do not do math anymore. I'm over it. I am above all that boorishness now.)

I explained to my son that I was indulging in a little hyperbole to make a point.

His comeback: "Only you would turn this into a conversation about a literary device, Mom."

My response: "I'm pleased you recognize the term, son. I believe my work here is done."

While it is true that I was trying to make a point about the perils of driving, I was happy to make a U-turn into a conversation about hyperbole. I hardly ever get to do that.

I have also been known to show my children gory accident-scene photographs, commercials, and PSAs. They certainly scare me to death, and I hope they scare my kids, too. I firmly believe that a healthy dose of fear is a good thing. It's one of my parenting premises. Guilt and fear have been used by countless generations of mothers to successfully parent their children. I am under no illusion that I am any better than the mamas who came before me. Bottom line: my primary goal in life is to keep my children alive to adulthood. I'll do almost anything to make that happen. Along the way, I want them to become educated, responsible adults, but ultimately those are just frills.

This reminds me of a conversation I had with an emergency-room physician at 2 A.M. when my son was having his first asthma attack.

"I'm worried about the side effects of that steroid," I told the doctor.

"If he can't breathe, he's going to die," the doctor responded.

I thought he made a darn good point.

I don't go about things quite like the Tiger Mom you've heard about in the news, but we certainly have common goals. I am living proof that being a mean mom works. My kids are turning out well. They have plenty of friends, but I'm not one of them. I'm way too busy being the mom. I am the first to admit that it is not always a fun job. If fear of me (or death) makes my kids think twice about speeding through neighborhoods, following too closely behind other cars, or talking and texting on their cell phones while they are driving, it will have been worth it.

I know full well that my teenagers have to make their own choices and live with the consequences. What I tell them over and over is that they should not let thirty seconds and one poor choice lead to a lifetime of regret. Our prisons are full of people who wish they'd made different decisions in the heat of the moment. It's so easy to do or say something that you can't take back! Teenagers face consequences for their actions that are beyond anything that we parents can protect them from. The penalty for one bad choice is sometimes death. I say these things over and over, as my kids will be quick to tell you. They know the standard lectures by heart. They often finish my sentences with me in a singsong voice. The gist is, "Yeah, yeah, yeah. We hear you." This is followed by bathroom doors slamming, earphones whipping over heads, and cars squealing away from the curb.

I once printed out the Alabama criminal statutes governing vehicular homicide and glued them to a poster. That's right. I made a visual aid and taped it on the mirror in my boys' bathroom.

That night, I overheard my middle son ask his older brother, "So, do you think she's calling us murderers now, or what?"

I barged right in to set the record straight. "No, no, *no!*" I said. "It's *potential* murder. This is what *could* happen to you, and your life would be ruined. And mine."

"And the person who died, Mom. They'd be in pretty bad shape, too," my older son pointed out wryly.

"Well, yes, of course. That, too," I admitted.

My boys stared at me after this exchange. They were obviously perplexed. In that particular parenting moment, we had no meeting of the minds. Some conversations go better than others. I'll be the first to admit that. The important thing is to never give up, no matter what. It's like working on a permanent peace for the Middle East. You can't give in. You have to continue searching for the most effective way to motivate your teens. I am constantly rooting around for carrots and sticks in my Mary Poppins bag of tricks. Occasionally, I'd like to reach for a baseball bat or a two-by-four. What can I say? I'm human.

I taught one teenager to drive. He's still breathing. So far, so good. I'm in the process of teaching another son to drive now. Like everything else I have experienced with my sons, teaching each of them to drive is a markedly different adventure.

My older son is overconfident, convinced he needs little supervision. "I got this," he often says to me. "You need to relax. You make me nervous when you cling to the dashboard with your fingernails like that."

My middle child is more cautious, as is his nature. He once woke us up in the middle of the night to confess, "I'm worried about something."

"What?" we asked, bleary-eyed with fatigue.

"I don't think I'm going to be a very good driver."

"Well, we've got some time to work on it, since you're only ten years old. But what makes you think that?"

"In my racecar video game, I crash all the time."

"It will be different with a real car," we promised him.

He wasn't totally convinced. I could tell.

When it came time for him to drive a real car, he was more cautious than his brother. When he tucked his six-foot-one frame behind the wheel, he hunkered down like he was afraid of being crushed by a meteor at any moment.

In a few years, I'll have to teach my daughter to drive, too. It's in the parenting contract. You have to teach *all* your kids to drive unless you can come up with a convincing reason not to. I haven't been able to think of anything to merit my excused absence. I've tried. The older I get, the more I dread this particular parenting job. I am more fearful with age. I want to warn my kids about tornadoes and credit card debt and cheating spouses and pyramid schemes. I feel like they are growing up at warp speed now, and I need to cram in every useful life lesson I've ever learned. I know it's not possible to do that. I just can't seem to help myself. I admit that it's not a pleasing dimension to my personality. I find myself taking every opportunity to teach my kids something, rather than simply enjoying experiences with them. The real problem is that I'm afraid I'm going to forget to teach them something they need to know to navigate the world without me.

I once told my husband that I thought I would be better at teaching the kids to drive if I could just have a quick toddy first. He thought that might not set the right tone for our lessons. I love the man, but sometimes he is such an Eagle Scout. It gets on my nerves.

One of the first things I do when teaching my kids to drive is to point out the differences in the general driving population. Teenage drivers assume everyone has twenty-twenty vision and quick reflexes simply because they themselves do. Of course, this isn't the case, not by a long shot. One simply must drive defensively. It takes time to develop those instincts, to just "know" when a car is about to pull out in front of you.

"How did you know he was going to pull out, Mom?" my son asked me one day.

"I'm not sure," I told him. "I just felt like he was going to do that, so I slowed down and left him some room."

"This is part of that witchy thing you have going on, isn't it?" he asked, staring at me with that speculative look in his eyes, like he was secretly wondering how I found out about the party he had gone to a few weeks before at a friend's house when the parents were out of town. What can I say? I had a feeling. I decided to do a drive-by and check out the party. He got busted.

"Probably. God gives moms a third eye to keep people like you in line," I said.

"Hilarious, Mom," he replied.

I know it is popular these days to tell kids that everyone can do everything equally well, but that is just a lie, and you and I both know it. Some of us are going to grow up to be astrophysicists. Others are going to work at the Jiffy-Mart. The good news is that we need all kinds to make our society work, so there's a place at the table for everyone, as far as I'm concerned. Some people are going to be better drivers than others. That's just the way it is. My husband is a better driver than I am. I hate to admit that because it's such a gender stereotype, but it happens to be true in our case. Teens realize quickly which of their friends are good drivers and which are not. I secretly use this information when working out carpools. It's very helpful.

Teenage drivers are on the steep side of the learning curve. They're going to bump into trash cans, mailboxes, and, unfortunately, other cars. It happens with frightening regularity. One of the smartest kids I know left his car in drive rather than putting it in reverse and plowed right smack into the back of his mother's car in his very own driveway *while she was sitting in her car*. I'm sure she wanted to beat him with the front bumper (which had fallen off during impact and was therefore quite handy), but the point is that she didn't. Every parent's hope is that any wrecks will be merely matters of property expense, rather than something worse. I promise you that every mother of a teenage driver checks her cell phone on a regular basis. We're all afraid. It comes with the territory.

I tell my children all the time, "Everyone can learn to drive defensively. It's simply a matter of education and experience." We are big on both of those virtues at our house. I also tell them honestly that some success in life is a matter of genetics. You play the hand you're dealt at birth. If you're five feet tall, there's no point in planning an NBA career. Pick another dream. That one is not going to happen. Driving isn't like that. With practice and a modicum of natural intelligence, anyone can learn to be a good driver. Well … almost everyone. There are exceptions to every generalization, of course.

You know what scares me most of all? Almost everyone has a driver's license. I am astonished by the variety of humanity that successfully passes the state driver's examination. How low can that bar possibly be? The next time you get your driver's license renewed, take a look around the DMV. Judging from the sea of humanity standing in line to get a new or renewed license, there is no requirement that a driver must be able to see through his or her hair. When my older son got his license, we stood in line behind a teenage girl who appeared to have only one eye. I suspect she had another one under those long bangs of hers, but I never actually saw it, so I can't say for sure. In my opinion, all that hair in the face would be a serious distraction. It was all I could do as a mother not to offer her a ponytail elastic from my purse. You need to be able to *see* to drive a car safely. That seems fairly bottom-line to me.

Most states do not have upper age limits for driving. That is a good news/bad news kind of thing. This means that it is up to each individual citizen to decide voluntarily when it is time to hang up the car keys. I was a little bit disappointed to find out about that when I was writing this chapter. Personally, I can't wait to tell my kids, "I'm too old to drive! One of you will have to come and get me!" Lord knows, I have schlepped them around for enough years. Even now, it is not uncommon for me to spend three hours a day in the car transporting my kids to and from their activities. I'd like a personal driver. I think that would be delightful. I don't know why Miss Daisy got so worked up. I'd volunteer to be driven around by Hoke right this very minute.

From my church pew on Sundays, I point out the wide variety of legal drivers in the general population to my kids: "See Mrs. So-and-so? She's still driving. She's ninety-two and has four cataracts. She's shrinking, too. There is no way she can see over the steering wheel. I know for a fact that she sits on a 1979 telephone directory for the city of Chicago. She's taken out every trash can on her street at least once. Watch out for her. And just so you know, you're taking your life in your hands if you park in front of the beauty shop where all the old ladies get their hair done every week."

I warn my kids that accidents often happen when people are in a hurry. Once when I was fifteen months pregnant with my youngest child and could no longer see my feet, which slowed me down considerably, I was loading groceries in my trunk in the parking lot of the Piggly Wiggly when a man leaned on his horn after deciding I was taking a little bit too long with my business. When the bag boy and I stared at him in open-mouthed astonishment, he went to town, hammering on his horn some more. He wanted my parking space, and he expected me to hop to it. I wondered what on earth he was in such a hurry for. I could only assume he was a brain surgeon and some poor soul was lying in mortal danger on the operating table unless he snagged my parking space and got what he needed at the Piggly Wiggly in one big hurry.

"There is no reason in the world to fight over a parking space," I tell my kids. "You're healthy. You can walk. People who fight over parking spaces to avoid walking an extra twenty yards are often the same people who have pricey gym memberships. And never allow yourself to be drawn into an argument with another driver, which can lead to road rage." My teenagers seem skeptical about that one. I can tell they think I made it up. "Happens all the time," I assure them smugly.

Teenagers and old people share the highways. If that doesn't put the fear of God in you, then nothing will. I can't think about it too much or I'll break out in hives. In addition, some people think nothing of sliding behind the wheel when they're exhausted, angry, depressed, or just plain drunk or high. Every single day, those drivers sail along the freeways alongside my teenagers and yours. It's enough to make me tell them to take the bus.

Distracted drivers are dangerous, too. For example, mothers often look back to minister to their children strapped into safety seats in the rear. I've certainly been there and done that. You've seen drivers engaged in heated arguments with passengers or someone at the other end of a cell phone call. You can easily recognize distracted drivers if you know what to look for. Anyone trying to eat a hamburger, smoke a cigarette, talk on a phone, and apply mascara simultaneously while driving a motorized vehicle falls into the unsafe driver category. You cannot expect those people to signal when they are turning or changing lanes because their hands are otherwise occupied.

As Professor Mad-Eye Moody urges Harry Potter and his friends, "Constant vigilance!" It's the only way to share the road with imbeciles and death-eaters, I suppose. Darwin was right, you know. I tell my teenagers that I do not want them to be involved in an accident caused by a human being weeded out during the process of natural selection.

No matter how many scary stories you cut out of the newspaper, forward from the Internet, share from your own youth, or make up on the spot, nothing will convince teenagers that driving is dangerous for them personally. That's because they can't imagine a world without them in it. I can't imagine that either. My mind goes totally blank at the thought of losing one of my children. It is my deepest fear. We grownups know too many real-life stories about teenagers losing their lives in car wrecks—the most likely way for them to die.

In young people's minds, the world really does revolve around them, so they can't foresee that making one bad choice while driving—failing to wear a seatbelt, texting, drinking—could cost their lives or someone else's. This is the reason that perfectly sane parents become hysterical when their kids are late for curfew or fail to check in when they arrive somewhere.

When a teenager cruises in at the last minute, oblivious to the agonizing hours his parents have been wondering whether he is dead or alive, he is also likely to say the one thing that will further inflame an already tense moment: "Chill, Mom. It's no big deal."

I have been known to say—and mean—"Lord, when that boy gets home, if he's okay, I may kill him myself."

You really must have lived through one of those long nights to appreciate that sentiment.

STRAIGHT FROM THE MOUTHS OF TEENAGE DRIVERS

1. "I'm not speeding! I'm going exactly the speed limit."

2. "That dent was already there."

3. "I'm not too close."

4. "That car needs to stay out of my lane."

5. "I know what to do. You told me that a hundred times already."

6. "I did come to a complete stop."

7. "This is harder than it looks."

8. "That was close!"

9. "Merging is hard."

10. "I forgot about crosswalks."

11. "I'm never going to parallel-park, so I don't need to practice that."

12. "You don't have to yell at me!"

13. "Sorry. Is that expensive to fix?"

14. "I drove well this time, didn't I, Mom? You didn't throw up once."

Who are You Talking To?

The first time I realized that my kids' world really is different from the one I grew up in started out like any other day. I began my morning by wading through debris in the basement in an attempt to get to my washing machine. My kids were out of school for the summer, and my basement looked like homeless people had been living in it for a couple of weeks. It smelled like it, too. I made a mental note to track down the odor of rotting meat and do something about it. I picked my way carefully through computer game disks (which cost fifty bucks each and were left scattered on the floor like chicken feed for kids to step on and crunch with their big teenage feet), candy wrappers, dirty socks, sofa pillows, wet swimsuits, headphones, magazines, empty water bottles, beach towels, and other trash. It looked like the day after a fraternity party or something you'd see on CNN after a tornado roared through.

By the time I reached my washer, I was already mad at my

teenagers. It wasn't even 7 A.M. As usual, the little trolls hadn't bothered to throw their half-eaten candy bars in the trash can. Someone's retainer was perched on the arm of a sofa. Gross. The television had been left on all night, of course, since my kids never turn it off when they leave the room. I run around after them every day turning off lights, stereos, and televisions. They waste enough electricity every week to power a small Caribbean island. They don't voluntarily tidy up after themselves ever. They don't clear away the half-empty soda cans, fluff the sofa cushions, or return their smelly tennis shoes to their rooms.

When my teenagers move on to other activities with their friends, they simply abandon their current trashed location like drug lords fleeing a narcotics raid. They just get up and go. It's inexplicable to me. I can track their activities throughout the day by walking from one mess to the next.

As I used both hands to randomly point, click, and wave the buffet of remote controls (which I found wedged between the sofa cushions) toward the television in search of silence and sanity, I realized that the screen showed a computer game in progress. It wasn't a television show at all. Then I noticed something unusual. In one corner of the screen, the names (pseudonyms, obviously) of the players were displayed. The bright blue screen said, "Afghanistan." That couldn't be right, could it? Was it possible that my kid was playing a computer game with the Taliban? If so, this was definitely bad. It would be a new low for us as a family. I decided I better look into the situation immediately.

"Son?" I called out at the top of my lungs in an effort to be heard in the kitchen upstairs, over the sound of ESPN's *SportsCenter*.

No one answered me, naturally. Teenagers have very selective hearing. They hear only what they want to hear. It's maddening. I picked up a broom, banged on the ceiling, and tried again.

"Son?"

"What?" a long-suffering voice responded.

"Ma'am? You mean *ma'am*, right?" I prompted for the millionth time.

"*Ma'am?*"

"Come here, please."

"What do you want?"

"Just come down here, please."

"Why?"

"Come. Down. Here. Now."

"I'm eating breakfast right now. I'll be down in a minute."

"*Get down here right this minute!*"

"*Okay!* You don't have to be such a grouch! What's the big deal, Mom?"

I pointed to the screen. "What is this, son?"

"I'm in the middle of a game," he said, as if any half-wit could have figured that out without help from him. "What did you think it was? I wasn't watching HBO! What are you mad about now?"

"Are you playing a live computer game with someone in *Afghanistan?*" I asked, incredulous.

"Yeah, I am. Cool, huh?" he said, flashing a grin at me and whipping the headphones from underneath the couch and putting them on his head. "I'm way ahead. See the points?"

I tried to maintain my composure. "*Who* are you talking to in Afghanistan?" I asked.

"I don't know, Mom. You can't see their real names."

"Let me get this straight. You are playing a game with an unknown person half a world away. Is that correct?" I asked.

"Sort of," he said, sensing I was about to launch into a lecture on Internet safety. He'd heard it all before—many, many times. He had no interest in an encore performance. "It's not a big deal, Mom. It's not dangerous or anything. Lots of my friends are playing live, too. We have teams."

"*Are you freakin' kidding me?*" I asked. "You could be playing with anyone! You could be playing a computer game with a terrorist!"

"I really doubt it, Mom. I don't think they're allowed to play computer games. It's probably one of our soldiers, actually. Anyway, you think everything is dangerous. You think pedophiles lurk everywhere on the Internet."

"They do! Pedophiles actively seek ways to reach you online! I'm not making this up!"

"Mom, you don't understand about this. It's okay. It's safe. Really. I'm six-one. I weigh 175 pounds. I think I can take the computer guy, Mom."

"*What?* Did someone ask to meet you in person?" I squealed. I was in full-alarm mode.

"*No!* I was *joking*, Mom."

We were at a technological impasse. It was one of many. Facebook. Twitter. Texting. Email. IMing. There's something new every single day. Sure, I read my kids' texts occasionally when I have their phones. I scroll through their computer's history to see where they've been. I enter as a friend occasionally on Facebook to see what my kids are posting (and what is being posted about them), but it's pretty random. I don't stalk my kids online like some parents I know. While I blow metaphorical raspberries at their right to privacy while they live under my roof, I don't really think I need to know all the teenage gossip. Nothing is worse than parents who are so involved in their kids' lives that they try to manage them like professional publicists. Tell the truth: do you really need to know all the cheerleader tittle-tattle? What good will come from that? The parents who do that scare me and my kids. Such behavior results in one thing and one thing only: a Lifetime movie of the week. Who wants to inspire one of those?

My kids came into the world reaching out with both hands. I love that about them. My oldest child used to lean forward in his umbrella stroller when we breezed through the mall. His arms would stretch as far he could reach, fingers spread wide open. He was literally grasping at life. He leaned forward to meet every new person, sight, sound, and experience. He was open to everything! He still is. As a mom, my instinct is always to be cautious, to take the safe bet, to look twice before leaping (feet first), and then to look one more time, just in case. "BecarefulIloveyousomuch" is my one-breath goodbye phrase whenever my kids walk out the front door.

When my middle child was four, he was obsessed with knights. We read stories about them every day. He wore a cape and carried a wooden sword all over the house. He had a prince, a castle, and a dragon painted on his wall. On his chest of drawers, I stenciled in gold, old-fashioned script, "Sir Nat, a true heart, a brave soul, a kind spirit."

In the middle of one of his adventures one afternoon, I cautioned him to be careful as he sailed over the top of the bunk beds in a frontal assault.

He paused for a moment, sword raised, and said, "You're not very brave, are you, Mom?"

"No, son, I'm not. I'm not a bit brave," I replied truthfully.

He considered for a moment, then said, "That's okay, Mom. I'll protect you."

Moms see danger everywhere. Boys do not. This is an important distinction.

I knew my older son was no longer a child one day when we were walking down the street side by side and a car swerved dangerously close to us. I remember thinking, *I better get my child out of the path of that car*, but before I could react, he shoved *me* out of the way and put himself in the path. It was a total role reversal, and it happened in less than a second, without any preplanning. It made me, the mean mama, cry, and I am not a weeper. (When we were at the movies one day, my daughter asked me why I don't cry at sad films like her friend's mom. When I just shrugged, she said, "I guess Virginia's mom is just nice." Yeah. I guess that explains it.)

My son was exasperated with my teary reaction. "What's the matter with you? That car didn't come close to hitting you!" he said.

It's not just the big milestones like birthdays and graduations that choke you up when you're a parent. Those are emotional moments, but you can see them coming. It's the little things that blindside you. You don't know when you read a book one night that it is the last time your kid will want to hear a bedtime story aloud. You have no idea when your daughter will suddenly say, "Thanks, but I can do my own hair. I don't need you to help."

I know I can't protect my teenagers from every threat. I do. But in general, that's the job: protect and defend. We're like the big blue line of police officers. Moms are the physical embodiment of 911. It's hard for teenagers to see any danger from cutting-edge technology. It isn't overt. The danger is hidden. And there are so many wonderful things about technology! I use Facebook, Twitter, and email every day of my life. It's part of the job these days if you are a writer like me. I'm lucky my kids can help when I get stuck.

The scary part about technology is that teenagers and adults approach social media very differently. I view such innovations with caution and suspicion, like a cat stalking a new vacuum cleaner. Teenagers push buttons without any thought whatsoever. They text with wild abandon while doing two or three other things at the same time. I know that forwarded emails, texts, and Facebook posts have ruined reputations, cost people their jobs, and been cited as evidence in divorce proceedings. I know that teenagers have bullied and been bullied online. My husband, a judge, has seen a huge increase in court records citing social network indiscretions. It's so quick! We've all sent emails in anger or by mistake and wished we could take them back two seconds later. Is there a more dangerous button on earth than *Reply to All?* That button should be red at the very least—the universal sign for danger and caution!

If I've said it once, I've said it a thousand times: once it's out there, it's out there forever. I tell my teens to imagine that every email they send will be copied to me, a teacher, a coach, or another parent. Believe me, if you write something that could get you in trouble, it will. If you would be ashamed for anyone to read it, you better not send it. Teenagers are just learning the rules of social interaction. They need the clues they get from other people's faces to learn what is and is not socially acceptable. It's hard to convey humor and tone in a text or email, even for professional humor writers like me. Just think how much harder it is for teenagers! How often have you heard teens say, "I was just kidding"?

My kids do not see any potential danger in the use of social media. The pace is fast and furious, and they imagine that their audience is always someone just like them. They don't think about the fact that every prospective employer is going to Google them. Colleges check out incoming students' online presences—fraternities and sororities do, too. No matter how many safeguards are built into the system, every piece of information you put out there can be used against you. My children think I'm a total kill-joy about the whole thing. So what else is new?

A common pitfall for teenagers is sexting. If you don't know what this is, you're lucky. I hope you never find out. This is a much more common phenomenon than you might think. (I find this prevalence hard to believe. Growing up, I never even called a boy on the telephone. I can't imagine sending a man a sexy text message. Clearly, I haven't lived a very interesting life. I become more aware of that every year. I have never even sent my husband a sexy text. If I did, there is no question in my mind what he would text back: "Who is this?" No one has ever sent me a sexy text either. The messages I receive say things like, "Come pick me up now" and "Don't forget the cat litter." Since sexting is apparently a rampant problem, I feel a little bit left out.)

"Sending a provocative or X-rated email may seem funny and cool when you envision your boyfriend or girlfriend reading it," I tell my kids, "but imagine that email being read by his or her parents. That happens all the time. How fun does that sound?"

Of course, there is no shoving all that stuff back in Pandora's box. Instant communication is part of our lives now, and there are good things about that, too. We don't have to wait for the five o'clock or ten o'clock news to find out what's going on around us. We get live news all day long on our phones, even. This technology saves lives. There's no question about that. The best we can do is to beg, bribe, order, and cajole our teenagers into using technology thoughtfully. They're going to make mistakes. Our job as parents is to minimize the collateral damage so they won't be sry when ppl LOL at them.

WWW.TEENAGER

1. No chat rooms. You don't need to talk to strangers about anything. Period.

2. Don't "friend" friends of friends! You have no idea where those people have been.

3. No sleeping with your cell phone. You don't need to be available twenty-four hours a day. You are not the president of the United States.

4. No, no, no, no, no texting and driving! You can wait until you reach your destination to confirm the nuclear launch codes.

5. No texting in church, at the dinner table, or at funerals or weddings.

6. Sometimes, you need to turn your cell phone off and be with real people. To be clear: Vibrate is not Off.

7. It's rude to text people when you are with someone else. Live people trump avatars every time.

8. It is just plain bad manners to send a thank-you text without a properly penned, snail-mailed follow-up. Don't even think about sending a condolence text. Break out your monogrammed stationery or invest in a Hallmark card from the drugstore.

9. Don't rat yourself out in a text. It's the equivalent of a written confession. Texts travel from person to person at the speed of light. Remember that. Forward is a one-button operation. Your mother is bound to see it.

10. Think before you text. Is it something you want floating around on your wedding day?

Leave a Light On, Please

hen I began writing this book, my teenagers and I hammered out a deal. Turns out, they are pretty tough negotiators. They agreed to be good sports about having their teenage angst paraded in front of the world for my professional shtick as long as I stayed away from one subject and one subject only. The topic they all agreed was taboo: dating.

"You cannot use the word *sex* in your book, Mom. Gross! You cannot speculate about the dating life of your teenagers. It's just too weird. Promise us right now you won't go there!" they demanded.

I agreed not to comment on the dating lives of the adolescents who live under my roof. It wasn't hard for me to take a vow of silence. I wasn't exactly anxious to head down that road myself. I'm a little bit of a prude.

Naturally, one of the first questions I received from my editor after he read the first draft of the book was, "Why isn't there a chapter about dating or sex in here?"

"Because my teenagers consider it an invasion of their privacy," I replied virtuously in my email response. I was thrilled to have a legitimate excuse to avoid that particular minefield. "Because I don't want to write a chapter about it," although true, doesn't sound nearly as professional.

Then I got to thinking. That almost always leads to trouble. Most often, I think thoughts like, *Why does she wear her hair like that?* or *I wonder if that's the woman he's having the affair with.* Most often, my thoughts do not merit sharing with readers. I rarely ponder world hunger or the current state of the economy or who's up for a Pulitzer Prize. Of course, I know perfectly well that dating is an important subject to address in a book like this. However, the idea of writing about it makes me want to put my head down on my desk. I am fully aware that ignoring the birds and bees accomplishes nothing. "Just say no" is a good idea. I'm all for it, but that doesn't mean I'm blind to the reality around me. "Everybody's human," the father of one of my friends always says. Temptation may have begun with a single man and woman in the Garden of Eden, but nothing much has changed since then. Half the drama incurred by teenagers is a result of raging hormones and a new awareness of the young men and women around them. Since I do not expect my daughter will want to join a convent nor my sons a monastery, I think that budding awareness is a good thing.

Teenagers have to learn how to interact with the opposite sex appropriately, respectfully, and responsibly. I think that modeling begins at home. Boys and girls observe how their fathers treat their mothers, and vice versa, and they tend to model their own treatment of the opposite sex based on those examples. The patterns tend to reappear across generations. We've all observed that. Dating etiquette really boils down to good manners. My kids will roll their eyes when they read that sentence. They know I savor nothing more than an opportunity to lecture on the importance of good manners in any endeavor.

I enjoyed watching my sons and later my daughter head out to their first dances in middle school. It was good practice. My daughter and her friends got together and preened in their party dresses. My boys donned freshly pressed slacks and button-down shirts and actually began to enjoy dressing up at that age. Corsages and boutonnieres were exchanged. Pictures were taken by beaming parents. The biggest question for sweaty-palmed boys was, "Will she say yes to a slow dance with me?" The biggest question for girls was, "What if nobody asks me to dance?" The good news these days is that girls often dance with one another, and big groups seem happy to take to the dance floor together.

Nothing quite prepares you for seeing your son or daughter clasped in the arms of a person of the opposite sex. It takes your breath away, literally. It's a bittersweet moment, one of those times you are reminded that this young person does not belong to you forever. That's how I felt, at least. I have a friend who chaperoned a dance with me and excused herself to go throw up. What can I say? You feel what you feel. When you actually see your son or daughter lock lips with a date, it's something else, let me tell you. It scrambles your brain for a few minutes.

When my boys started dating, I worried about everything. Would girls break their hearts? Would one of them break some girl's heart? Would they know how to behave in new, coed situations? Occasionally, I overheard in the car or when their friends came over (they almost never volunteer any love-life information to this day) that my boys were "going with" some girl or other. The names of the girls changed on a regular basis. There was obviously no real emotional investment. Gradually, I realized that those crushes were just part of the learning curve. My boys never actually went anywhere with the girls they were "going with." They rarely spoke to one another on the telephone or over the computer.

One day when I was sitting on the screened-in porch with one of my sons, I recognized his most recent crush jogging by our house with her father. "Isn't that So-and-so?" I asked.

"Yeah," he responded.

"Aren't you even going to speak to her?" I prodded.

"I'll see her tomorrow in school," he said.

"If I were a girl, that would hurt my feelings!" I said, baffled.

"You are a girl, Mom. You're just an old girl."

"Don't change the subject. You know what I mean," I said.

All in all, those years were a whole lot of nothing. They were good practice, though, for high school.

High-school dating is a different kettle of fish entirely. Things have changed a lot since I was in high school. Teenagers generally travel in packs nowadays. You don't see as much one-on-one dating. I kind of like that. It's hard to get into trouble in front of a big group of friends. There's safety in numbers, and I mean that in all the ways that you can think of and probably a few more that you can't if you don't yet have teenagers.

One reason kids don't date as much as they used to is because it is so darn expensive. Taking a girl to a movie is a forty-dollar evening these days. Tickets are nearly ten bucks each. Two small drinks and popcorn, and those boys are looking at dropping half a month's allowance in one night. That's pretty steep. One of my boys came home after one of his first dates outraged that his companion for the evening "ordered the most expensive thing on the menu!" Another reason you see kids going out in big groups is that it allows those who are self-confident to smooth the way for their friends who are a bit shy around members of the opposite sex. That's kind, I think.

Eventually, of course, one of your children falls in love. It happens to everyone with reassuring regularity. All the classic signs appear. It's more than a crush. You can see it's the real deal, at least for the moment. From a parent's point of view, it's a whole new ball game. You have to bite your tongue to keep from spouting constant dire warnings like some Greek oracle of doom and gloom. As an adult, you can see the inevitable heartbreak on the horizon, but you can't protect your teenager from the experience. It's all part of growing up.

No one is more irritating to take on a family vacation than a teenager in love. At that moment in time, blood ties mean nothing. No one is more important in that teen's world than the girlfriend or boyfriend who is being left behind. There's nothing quite like spending a small fortune on a family getaway only to have your lovelorn teenager mope through the week. The good news is that love interests wax and wane. As a parent, it's best not to get too involved. You don't want to know too much about who "likes" whom. It's not your business. Plus, the cast of characters is constantly changing like something out of the Swinging Sixties. My motto: be nice to all of them. You never know who may end up with their feet under your table at Thanksgiving dinner. Your future sons-and daughters-in-law are out there somewhere right now. Think about that. I sure hope their parents are doing a good job. Somebody else's kids are going to be my grandchildren's parents! That's the kind of thought that keeps me up at night.

On the outside, teenagers look a lot more sophisticated these days. I don't know if it's the new dermatology drugs, better vita-mins, or exposure to a world of information through the Inter-net, but the girls my boys date look like college-aged beauties. I've seen them in prom dresses that cost more than my entire winter wardrobe. I've watched seventeen-year-old girls stride confidently on three-inch heels that would toss me into a flower bed in mere seconds. Prom night is an extravaganza that rivals wedding-party events. There are limousines, major photography sessions, expen-sive dinners, breakfasts afterward, and expensive formal wear. If you're the parent of a boy in this scenario, let's just say you're in for big bucks. I'm looking forward to being on the girl end of that evening with my daughter!

When I was my daughter's age, I looked like it. We wore knee socks and loafers, and I had bushy caterpillar eyebrows. It could have been worse. I had a friend who looked like she was grow-ing a handlebar mustache. Back then, I had never heard of anyone who had her eyebrows or upper lip waxed, but as a brunette with porcelain-pale skin, I sure could have used some salon help. Not many girls wore makeup or nail polish either, and if they did, it was inexpertly applied and a little daring. I was a full-grown wom-an before I ever had a manicure or pedicure. Now, little girls do that at birthday parties!

Times have changed. Human nature has not. Boys like girls. Girls like boys. Occasionally, boys like boys and girls like girls. It can get confusing. These days, I feel like a professional chaperon. It's a big part of my current job description. "All your friends are welcome in our house," I tell my teenagers, but when we entertain boys and girls together, we observe some general rules of decorum.

1. No sitting around in the dark. Leave a light on, please.

2. Couples will remain upright on couches and chairs. No reclining.

3. My husband and I will make periodic passes through the living room, basement, porch, and any other areas where teenagers congregate, just to keep everyone on the up-and-up.

Teenagers in my house are under my supervision, so I feel free to offer correction on an as-needed basis. I try to be nice about it. In exchange, I offer unlimited soft drinks, pizza, and other snacks. I also promise to make my evening patrols mere drive-bys. I speak politely to my kids' friends, indulge in a few minutes of chitchat, and then go about my business. I genuinely try not to embarrass anyone. That is sometimes hard. By the time midnight rolls around, I'm exhausted and ready for bed. I'm sporting mismatched sweats and T-shirt, and I've usually washed the makeup off my face and substituted my out-of-date glasses for contacts. I can be quite a vision of beauty when I come down those stairs to "do laundry" at eleven o'clock at night. I also ask that all children who enter and leave my home greet me or my husband and tell us they are leaving, so that we know who is actually on the premises. Nothing is more embarrassing than when a parent calls and asks, "Is So-and-so there?" and I say, "No, haven't seen him tonight," and then have to call back and report, "He's in my basement—I didn't know." That does not make me a happy camper.

One day, I want to have those precious grandchildren I always hear so much about. The point is that I want them way, way down the line, after everyone is well educated and able to support themselves and their dependents.

Bottom line: I tell it like it is. I think that is the only way to live with teenagers without losing your mind. I often say, "I'm old and tired. I am not rearing any more children in this house! Got it?"

THE MOM CHAPERON

1. Teen: "We broke up."
   Mom: "It would have been nice to know that before I ran into her mother at the grocery store."

2. Teen: "Try not to talk to my date too much while I finish getting dressed."
   Mom: "No problem. Would you prefer we sit in the living room in silence?"

3. Teen: "I'm going to wait outside for my date to pick me up."
   Mom: "You are not a FedEx package. Your date must come to the door, knock, and be introduced."

4. Teen: "I like her a lot, but I can't stand her mother."
   Mom: "Just FYI, you probably wouldn't like her any better as a mother-in-law."

5. Teen: "She's really, really, really pretty."
   Mom: "I don't think you heard the question, son. I asked you what you like about her."

6. Teen: "He is so cute! I can't just go up and talk to him!"
   Mom: "So you're saying that if he were ugly you could talk to him without all the drama?"

7. Teen: "We've been dating for six whole weeks!"
   Mom: "I guess it's time to introduce him/her to all the cousins, then."

8. Teen: "I can't wear that on a date!"
   Mom: "Why? Because it is tasteful and appropriate and you look charming in it?"

9. Teen: "I can't get my hair cut right before the dance!"
   Mom: "I see. Well groomed is bad, right?"

10. Teen: "I don't want to go to the party with a date if you have to drive us."
    Mom: "Would you prefer to take a cab?"

The Rebuttal

Dear Reader,

You cannot believe everything you read. You've heard only one side of the epic *Parent v. Teenager* battle in this book: the mother's side, *my* mother's side. I know her pretty well. Believe me, she's not telling you everything. There's more to the story. You have to consider context. Since people my age have yet to gain a foothold in the world of publishing, I can only assume that angry teenagers are an under-represented demographic. With this is mind, I take personal satisfaction in writing a small rebuttal to this book-long harangue of my people. Obviously, my mom was on a tear in these pages. That's something to see in person, let me tell you. You do not want to be on the listening end of one of my mother's lectures when she's in a mood. It's best to apologize quickly. If you let her get a full head of steam, there's no stopping her, and you could be trapped for hours listening to her go on and on about the same old stuff.

First of all, I would like to express my shock and dismay at the amount of name-calling in my mother's most recent literary work. I note that she frequently uses nouns like *wretch, sneak, troll,* and *rodent* to describe the delightful children she gave birth to. I ask you, is that nice? I think that's actually preteen behavior, don't you? Very immature, Mother.

Although most of the unbelievably many gripes and grievances my mother writes about in this book are factually accurate, my counterarguments and those of my siblings are not given even token representation. I assure you that if we'd told you the same stories, we'd look a lot better in them.

Let me mention a few things about my mother. First of all, our household is proof that Kim Jong-il is on to something with that whole absolute dictator thing. Mama's rules are the law around here, and the rules are apparently subject to change with or without the approval of the actual state judicial representative who lives under the same roof. Our dad really is a judge, but he's not nearly as scary as Mom. The Bill of Rights means nothing in these walls. Censorship is tight. Verbal chastisement is constant. Punishments can consist of certain jobs that may fall under the category of biological terrorism (see the story about my cleaning the porch).

Think about this for a minute: adults always talk about wanting to relive their college days, but no one ever says they wish they could relive high school. I know why. Teenagers like me have no control over anything in our everyday lives. It's so frustrating! We don't get much sympathy either. In our world, every part of our day consists of situations where we are treated like inferior beings or second-class citizens, people who need to be bossed around. Teachers make us read about irrelevant and monotonous subjects whether we are interested in a career involving research on electromagnetism or not. After school, coaches bark in our ears for three hours in the hot sun and give us orders in the rudest manner possible. When we come home, we are expected to be pleasant when our parents order us around in an even more hostile tone than the coaches! Excuse me, Mom, if I don't leap to put up the clothes that seem pretty indifferent as to whether they are stored on the floor or in the dresser.

While I am on the subject of dictators and their orders, let me summarize my ideas about the way curfews are handled around here. Like communism, curfews are a good idea in principle, but the practice just manages to tick everyone off. Sometimes, two parents give different times to be home. They don't always check with each other. Parents often seem to forget the deal we made about the curfew before I left for the night, or they give vague, confusing instructions like, "Don't be home too late." What does that mean? My parents may be getting Alzheimer's. They are *old*. I have an advantage in remembering exactly what was said in earlier conversations because my brain is still young and sharp.

Unfortunately, I have learned that no matter how well one does in the opening arguments with parents, their closing statements always result in a guilty verdict for teenagers. This constant cloud of defeat probably contributes to teenagers' frequently unpleasant and angry attitudes that my mother complains about (over and over again). Here's the perfect analogy: imagine playing baseball all your life and never winning one game, even though you took some teams into extra innings!

It's not easy being a teenager, no matter what my mom says. You realize that parents are legally obligated to pay for our food, clothes, and living expenses, right? We didn't ask to be born. I say take it up with the Supreme Court, but don't grumble about it to us. I'm sure someone told my parents long ago that those sweet, innocent babies would at some point turn into big, hairy, mean teenagers. I think adolescence is like boot camp right before you go to real war. It's hard on everybody.

In a short time, I will be leaving for college. There are a few things I will miss about my teenage years under this roof. I will miss my brother and sister. I'll miss my mom's pound cake and my dad taking us to Alabama football games. My mother says I will miss the clean clothes that will no longer appear in my room, too. I may even miss my parents—the dictator and the judge.

Seriously, when I have kids, I hope I am as good a parent as my parents have been for me. I'm talking about the kids I have in the distant, distant future, as I am sure my mom was thinking when she read that sentence—which is just the kind of thing to crank her up on a sex-education discussion.

Sincerely,

Warner Thompson

ACKNOWLEDGMENTS

At the end of every statewide campaign, it is customary for politicians like my husband to give flowery, over-the-top speeches thanking the volunteers and paid staff who work behind the scenes to ensure their candidate's success. It is a running joke in our household that I refuse to be thanked publicly by my husband. I don't need public recognition for that. I support him because I love him. For goodness' sake, I've been married to the man for twenty-five years. That number speaks volumes. I respect his work, and I think Alabama is lucky to have him on the appellate bench. However, he knows full well that if he ever plants a big, wet kiss on my lips in front of an audience, he's going down for the count. I mean it. The very idea makes me nauseated.

Every time I finish writing a book, I find myself in the same position as those post-campaign politicians. I *want* to thank people. Like me, most of them would rather not be thanked. They help me because they love me. Isn't that lovely?

So . . . regardless of the consequences, I have a few individuals I want to thank in these pages. Since this is my book, I can do what I want.

This time, thanks especially to Vera and Rip Britton and Whitney Page. These friends read late-night, frantic emails with strange subject lines like, "Quick! Quick! Read this and tell me if it's funny or not!" They mulled over things, encouraged me, and gave me wise counsel. I couldn't ask for finer friends.

Thanks to Vicki Johnson, who dragged me kicking and screaming—no modest feat—into the world of social media. That woman has the patience of a saint. She even laughed when I accidentally invited my Episcopal bishop, Kee Sloan, to be my friend on Facebook. Even better, she used her nimble fingers to fix it. She's my kind of gal.

A special thank-you to Renea Lucy for taking the photograph of my kids—twenty minutes and no one screamed!

As always, thanks to my personal photographer, Brit Huckabay. Brit can make any woman look good and feel like a rock star. Feel free to book a photo session with him yourself. You'll see what I'm talking about.

Big news: I worked with a new editor on this book, Steve Kirk. You all know how much I love change (not at all), so I'm sure I was a little party for him. All I can say is, "Steve, you are so *the man*." This book is infinitely better than it would have been without him. I now know why he has that "senior editor" title. A great editor is like a wife (or so I imagine). Steve gets my heartfelt gratitude and a pound cake. Lord knows, he earned it.

As always, thanks to the home team—husband, children, parents, sister, and friends—for making it possible for me to write what I love, travel to speaking events, and still keep my day job as mother and dictator. I love you all.